Franklin B. Gardner

The Painters' Almanac for the Half-Years of 1879 and 1880

THE
Painters' Almanac

FOR THE

Half-years of 1879 & 1880.

Calculated for the use of Carriage, Wagon and Car Painters in all parts of the Temperate Zone.

By Dr. Franklin.

NEW-YORK:
FRANKLIN B. GARDNER, Publisher,
Franklin Square.

Franklin B. Gardner

The Painters' Almanac for the Half-Years of 1879 and 1880

ISBN/EAN: 9783337337476

Printed in Europe, USA, Canada, Australia, Japan

Cover: Foto ©Thomas Meinert / pixelio.de

More available books at **www.hansebooks.com**

PREFACE.

In presenting a detailed description of the various operations necessary to complete a first-class job of Carriage-painting, I am aware that I take upon myself a heavy task, and that my statements are liable to be adversely criticised by some of the craft. But I feel that my endeavors to shed light in some dark corner of the Paint-shop will be appreciated by a majority of my readers, and particularly by those who know the difficulties which environ the writer on technical subjects.

"The American Method of Carriage-painting" is now admitted to be the one which gives the best satisfaction, by the leading Carriage-builders of this country and of Europe, and its adoption in their workshops gives further evidence of their appreciation of its fitness for the very best work. Therefore it is to this Method that I shall call particular attention in the following pages.

It must be noted, however, that although a Daily Record is given of WHAT TO DO to produce eminently superior work by this Method, there are many roads leading to the same point or destination; and those who prefer "rapid transit" to the more staid and homely means of reaching that point, may please their fancy without impairing, in any great degree, the result they aim to produce. I shall, possibly, lay out a "rapid transit" mode of Painting a Carriage or Sleigh ere the three hundred and thirteen working-days of this Almanac are completed, but in entering upon the work my desire is to show how to Paint a job in the BEST manner.

My experience in the working of this system, and the exertions made to bring it to a successful issue, while holding a prominent position in the Painting Department of Brewster & Co., (of Broome-st.,) New York, together with extended journeyings among the Carriage-shops of the United States, has given me the means of knowing whereof I speak, and my aim has been to correctly write out such knowledge, hoping that it would at least merit a careful study by the apprentice, and perhaps be the means of guiding some fellow-workman into a path more thickly strewn with roses than with thorns.

FRANKLIN B. GARDNER.

1879   JULY.   1879

"When others do your work excel,
Then strive to do your work as well."

Sun.	Mon.	Tue.	Wed.	Thu.	Fri	Sat.
- -	- -	1	2	3	4	5
6	7	8	9	10	11	12
13	14	15	16	17	18	19
20	21	22	23	24	25	26
27	28	29	30	31	- -	- -
- -	- -	- -	- -	- -	- -	- -

Tuesday, 1.

ONE THING AT A TIME.

When starting in life for yourself, my boy,
  Be careful how you begin ;
Oh, don't be too anxious for gain, my boy,
  Or else you never will win.

One thing at a time is enough to do,
  But see that it is in your line ;
Remember the adage, as old and true—
  Too many clusters break the vine.

Wednesday, 2.

Preparations are now being made to celebrate the Anniversary of the Independence of the United States on the 4th, and it is one of the standing rules in all well-regulated shops, that a general cleaning-up shall be made, particularly in the paint-shop, and care be taken that

JULY, 1879.

all inflammable substances shall be well stored away in safe places; that all broken panes of glass shall be repaired, in order to prevent the entrance of fire-works through the carelessness of the fire-cracker brigade, and that there be as little unfinished work on hand as possible.

Thursday, 3.

No MAN ever finished his work, for each task is but a preparation, which, being completed, should be put under our feet, that we may thenceforward labor on a higher level. Thus, no true worker was ever satisfied with what he accomplished, for by doing that he had qualified himself to do something better.

Friday, 4.

Independence Day: let it be celebrated in a joyful manner, but do not enter into the festivities with such vigor and in such a manner that thy morrow will be o'ershadowed by pains which rack thy brain or cause thee to regret thy doings upon this glorious Fourth.

Saturday, 5.

This day being the last one of the broken week, why not devote the time to thoughts of the future? Prepare for a new era in your shop. Look about you, and you find your competitors in trade are improving. They possibly have adopted the modern way of doing work. "The American Method of Carriage-painting" has been proved a success, and why not adopt it? To aid you in carrying out the method, we append hereto full and explicit directions for each day's work. beginning with

Monday, 7.

Begin to-day by applying to a new body a coat of Permanent Wood Filling. Lay the material on with a clean brush, then immediately wipe off all you can with clean rags, leaving none on the surface, as in a coat of paint or varnish. Paint the parts inside the body which are canvassed, with slush paint.

Tuesday, 8.

This day may be given for the drying of the P. W. F., and if it is a damp day keep the job in a warm room, otherwise place it in the sun

JULY, 1879.

and air. The woodwork of the gears may now be coated with P. W. F. and wiped off in the same manner as the body, after which they may be sent to the smith-shop to be ironed.

Wednesday, 9.

The body having stood in a good drying atmosphere, is now ready for a coat of Valentine's Ground Roughstuff. Use this material just as it comes from the maker, excepting in this first coat a very little raw oil may be added to give it the required elasticity; thin to a working consistency with turpentine, and lay on smoothly.

Thursday, 10.

The coat of roughstuff now being dry, we may putty up all nail-holes and imperfections in the surface with putty made as follows: Take equal portions of dry white-lead and whiting in bulk (not weight) and add one-half the quantity of keg-lead (lead ground in oil). Mix them together by pounding with a wooden mallet, using as a thinning or mixing liquid equal parts of Crown Coach Japan and rubbing varnish. This putty will harden in twelve hours, and is not apt to shrink or crumble from out the holes.

Friday, 11.

The putty being dry and the roughstuff coat well hardened, the *second* coat of roughstuff is now in order. Apply the roughstuff without the addition of oil this time; simply thin it a little with turpentine. It is a good plan to lay the roughstuff across the grain of the previous coat, and care should be taken that no brush-marks be left in the work, for they will certainly show in the finish. The roughstuff must be laid evenly and as smoothly as it can be to bring about good results.

Saturday, 12.

You may let the smith take the body to-day, to hang it up and fit irons, and as he will probably keep it in his department two days, we will have ample time, in the absence of other work, to take a retrospective view and see what we have accomplished.

JULY, 1879.

Monday, 14.

The priming coat of P. W. F. on the body has closed the pores of the wood against the entrance of all other liquids, although it does not appear to have done so. We know by experiment and tests that dampness will not enter the wood, neither will the oils from subsequent coats be absorbed, and surely that is a strong point in favor of durability.

Tuesday, 15.

The coat of P. W. F. put upon the wheels, beds, bars, etc., of the gears, was done as a protection against the oils, smoke and water of the smith-shop, and we call it the "preventive coat." It will eventually be cut off with sandpaper. It is very beneficial to the work, and should not be neglected.

Wednesday, 16.

The carriage being ironed, now returns to the paint-shop, where it is filed and sandpapered until the whole is clean and smooth. You should remember that the better the condition of the job at this stage, the better the finish will be, and less labor will be necessary to finish it.

Thursday, 17.

All smoked or burned places on the body being scraped clean, the third coat of roughstuff may now be applied, using the mixture as it comes from the manufacturer, excepting the thinning with turpentine, to have it work easily. The gears are now ready for the priming coat of P. W. F., which should be put on over wood and iron alike, then well wiped off with clean rags.

Friday, 18.

The fourth and last coat of roughstuff is now in order. The P. W. F. on gears having stood forty-eight hours is now quite dry, and you may now putty over any open-grained places or other imperfections with soft putty. Late in the afternoon a coat of "staining" (yellow ochre or Indian red) may be put over the roughstuff.

JULY, 1879.

Saturday, 19.

It will be best to allow the body to stand to-day for the roughstuff to harden. The gears may be lightly sandpapered over the parts puttied, and to insure the surface against absorption, a light coating of P. W. F. should be given, particularly over the putty, and the whole well wiped off with clean rags.

Monday, 21.

Select some good pumice-stone lumps and "rub the body out of roughstuff," after which allow it to stand at least eight hours (or over night) for the water to evaporate from the porous roughstuff surface. The gears are now ready for *color;* and after dusting them well apply the color (say lampblack) with a camel's-hair brush.

Tuesday, 22.

The body being dry, apply a thin coat of P. W. F. to the rubbed surface, to close up the pores of the roughstuff; wipe off very carefully and stand the job aside to dry. The gears may now be "mossed off" and have the second coat of color (ivory black) laid on with a camel's-hair brush.

Wednesday, 23.

Gently rub the surface of the body with the back of a piece of sandpaper: dust off and apply a "ground" coat of lampblack. The gears may now receive black color-and-varnish; lay it on plentifully and "dress" it as well as if it were a finishing coat; besides, keep it as clean as possible, to save labor in future operations.

Thursday, 24.

This day should be devoted to coloring the body and getting the irons and loose pieces in proper order, to keep up with the rest of the job. The gears are left to dry in a clean place. Late in the afternoon the first coat of Black Japan, or color-and-varnish, may be put upon the body, using good varnish-brushes for the work.

JULY, 1879.

Friday, 25.

Black Japan is considered best for all black work, although some who are unaccustomed to it prefer color-and-varnish. The Japan makes a deeper jet black, and sets off any color that comes in close connection with it. It sets quickly, and must be handled in a lively manner—a knack easily learned. Too much "dressing" injures the work.

Saturday, 26.

The body should now be lightly rubbad with pulverized pumice-stone and water, and receive a coat of Black Japan having about five per cent. of hard-drying body-varnish added to it. The gears may now be rubbed down with pumice-stone and water, and be striped.

Good stripers, as a general rule, give the preference to flat or "dagger" striping pencils, and say that they can do better work with them. If you have never used these pencils you will no doubt have some difficulty with them at first; but *nil desperandum;* practice until you can handle them at will.

Monday, 28.

Now rub the body and prepare it for the third and last coat of Black Japan or color-and-varnish, adding, say, ten per cent. of hard-drying body-varnish to the Japan. This renders it more elastic, and also tends to make it work better under the brush. In rubbing the Black Japan surface you may "cut through," and in order to "touch up" such places, first coat them with dead-quick black, then glaze over with ordinary asphaltum (purchased at the nearest paint-store) thinned with turpentine, which will give the jet black color of the Japan.

The gears may now be washed off and receive a medium heavy coat of Elastic leveling varnish.

Tuesday, 29.

The body may now be taken in hand by the trimmer, and he will probably require one day to complete his work.

Wednesday, 30.

The body having returned from the trimming-shop, dust off and give it a careful rubbing with pumice-stone; wash clean, then rub over again with fine rotten-stone and water, touch up any bare places, and apply the finishing coat of Valentine's Wearing Body Varnish. Rub off gears and finish them by flowing on a coat of Valentine's Elastic Gear Varnish. We have shown that a piece of work may be done in a first-class manner inside of four weeks, and in the same manner a heavy job—say a landau worth twenty-five hundred dollars—may be done; the only difference would be the smith and the trimmer would require a longer time in which to complete their work.

Thursday, 31.

Give this day for the varnish to harden, which, providing your varnish-room is supplied with a ventilator, will go on rapidly and well. Keep the temperature of your room up to about 75 degrees Fahrenheit. You may then "hang up" the job, "black off" bolt-heads, etc., and run it into show-room when "blacking off" is dry, wash off the whole job with clean cold water, dry well with a clean shammy, and the work is done.

ADVANCEMENT will probably come to you far more slowly than your aspirations. Almost all permanent good is of slow growth. The coral-workers build up their massive islands grain by grain. One of the world's distinguished workers had this picture hanging upon his wall where his eye could often rest upon it: Only a man with his coat off, a pick in his hand, with which he was delving away at the base of a mountain, and below it this motto, "Little by little." Take this for *your* motto, and never fear but the mountain of difficulty will give way before your persistent strokes.

THE VARIOUS PROCESSES detailed as above are plainly shown by a "Chart," published by Messrs. Valentine & Company, which will be sent on application to them.

This Chart gives the "slow" and "quick" methods of painting bodies, gears, and sleighs.

1879 AUGUST. 1879

Never let your reputation tarnish
By doing your work with common varnish.

Sun.	Mon.	Tue.	Wed.	Thu.	Fri.	Sat.
--	--	--	--	--	1	2
3	4	5	6	7	8	9
10	11	12	13	14	15	16
17	18	19	20	21	22	23
24	25	26	27	28	29	30
31	--	--	--	--	--	--

Friday, 1.

NIL DESPERANDUM.

Work with a will: half-way efforts are futile;
When a task is before you, with zeal "buckle to;"
'Tis only by earnest and steady endeavor
You can fitly accomplish the object in view.

Work with a will, for in life there's no station
So lowly that Industry cannot adorn;
'Tis honored by all whose esteem is worth having;
They dishonor themselves who dare treat it with scorn.

Saturday, 2.

This month is generally the hottest of the year in the United States, and the finisher is frequently troubled with the deviltries caused by excessive heat, such as sweating, pitting pinholing. etc. The varnish-room should be well ventilated, either by ventilators in the windows or by a pipe running through the ceiling and roof, or the amount of oxygen in the room will be insufficient to *harden* the varnish.

Monday, 4.

MIXING COLORS.—It is the custom of many painters when about to put several pigments together to form a desired color, to mix the dry pigments upon the stone into one mass and then grind them in the mill; and it is frequently by this means that dull or "lifeless" colors are produced. To produce perfect colors, let the painter mix and grind into separate cups the pigments required to make the color wanted, and then add one to the other until the desired shade or tone of color is produced. By this means all the freshness of the color will be retained, a more perfect commingling of the particles will be insured, and there will be less liability of separation, or the settling of one heavy pigment from the others in the cup, which is so sure to destroy the uniformity of coloring.

Tuesday, 5.

DESERVE friends and you will have them. The world is teeming with kind-hearted people, and you have only to carry a kind, sympathetic heart in your own bosom to call out goodliness and friendliness from others. It is a mistake to expect to receive welcome, hospitality, words of cheer, and help over rugged and difficult passes in life, in return for cold selfishness, which cares for nothing in the world but self.

Wednesday, 6.

IMPROVING CARRIAGE-TOPS.—The best preparation in use for dressing or refinishing old leather carriage-tops is Valentine's Enameled Leather Varnish. It is a thin, black dressing, and may be applied to the leather with an ordinary paint-brush. The leather should first be well washed with Castile soap and water to remove grease, and to soften it; then a single application of the varnish will give the top the appearance of a new one, and in half an hour it may be run out into the street.

AUGUST, 1879.

Thursday, 7.

A GENTLEMAN caught a negro carrying off some of his fancy poultry the other night. "What are you doing with my chickens?" he yelled. "I wuz gwine fer ter fetch 'em back, boss. Dere's a nigger 'round here what's been 'sputin' longer me 'bout dem chick'ns. I sed dey wuz Coachin' Chyniz, an' he sed dey wuz Alabamer pullits, an' I wuz jist takin' 'em fer ter 'stablish my nollege. Dey don't lay no aigs, does dey, boss? Ef dey does, I'm mighty 'shamed er hustlin' uv 'em 'round. Aigs is scase."

Friday, 8.

GREASY COLOR.—It is sometimes the case that a coat of rubbing-varnish crawls or enamels on some colors, while on others it does not do so. The cause is due to what is known among painters as "greasy color;" that is, the color, if not mixed with oil, is in itself of a greasy nature, and drying with a smooth, oily surface, the varnish does not readily adhere to it. By simply washing or wiping this greasy color with a damp shammy no trouble will be experienced.

Saturday, 9.

How pleasant it is to be able to be independent of others and able to manage your own affairs in your own way! You feel some satisfaction in having accomplished something by your own unaided efforts, and if you go on trying to improve, success is sure to follow. In this world of gain good judgment is an important matter, and it is gained by earnest study and the habit of *seeing* whatever one looks at.

Monday, 11.

CLEAN VARNISH-CUPS.—It is next to impossible to put on a clean coat of varnish when a cup that is covered both inside and out with old gummy and partially dried varnish is used for holding it. Every time the brush is wiped over the edge some of the old gum will be removed and at last be found upon the work. Varnish-cups should be left in a bath of strong potash-lye until every particle of varnish is eaten off, then rinsed in clean water and dried with a clean shammy.

AUGUST, 1879.

Tuesday, 12.

It is false economy to work all night and remain in bed for hours the next morning, when if you retire at a seasonable time you will gain a good night's rest, and arise refreshed and ready to commence work in the bright sunlight, which is far better than any artificial illumination that can be produced. If you hear of persons complaining that they are no better off at the end of the year for all their economy, you may, as a general thing, conclude that the economy they have been practising is not the true kind.

Wednesday, 13.

A WORLD WITHIN ITSELF.—Every varnish-room should be provided with a *thermometer* and a *barometer;* the former to indicate the temperature of the room, the latter to show when a change in the weather is likely to occur; and with these two tell-tales hung upon the wall the varnisher may so regulate the climate or atmosphere of the room—providing he has the necessary heating and ventilating arrangements—as to make it, as the saying is, "a world within itself."

Thursday, 14.

"Money never made a man happy yet, nor will it. There is nothing in its nature to produce happiness. The more a man has the more he wants. Instead of its filling a vacuum it makes one. If it satisfies one want, it doubles and trebles that want another way. That was a true proverb of the wise man—rest upon it: 'Better is little with the fear of the Lord than great treasure and trouble therewith.'" —*Franklin.*

Friday, 15.

THE VARNISH-ROOM FLOOR.—The best floor yet devised for a varnish-room is one made of pine plank, double-laid, and having a gentle incline from one side to the other; then on the lowest side a sort of gutter should be made to lead off water through a pipe or pipes to the outer world. This floor should be *well painted* with refuse paint from the shop, commonly known as "slush." This serves to prevent absorption of water by the floor, and thus overcomes, in most cases, that "deviltry" known as "pitting." A floor covered with tin or zinc is objectionable, owing to the liability to puncture it with irons or sharp-edged tire.

Saturday, 16.

It is certainly a fact that some people can make money "go farther" than others; that is, they can procure more comforts for a given sum expended than their neighbors. A man in New York, recently, with one dollar, got a shave, a breakfast, a paper collar, a pack of cigarettes, had lunch, beer, dinner for two, consisting of soup, fish, maccaroni with cheese, beefsteak, apples and peanuts, attended a concert, got lodging for the night and a cup of coffee in the morning, and had five cents left, with which he purchased a ticket on the Elevated Railroad and went eight miles to Harlem.

Monday, 18.

BLACK JAPAN.—Black Japan, which is used in the place of color-and-varnish upon the black portions of a carriage, is a perfect jet black, and far superior in every respect to ivory black or color-and-varnish. It is quite "quick-drying," and in order to make first-class work with it the painter must understand its peculiarities, one of which is this "quick-setting" quality, necessitating a rapid movement of the brush; but the "knack" of handling this material once learned, we feel assured no return to ordinary color-and-varnish will be made, and no trouble will be experienced in laying it off, providing the painter operates the brush in a lively manner, making no more motions with the hand than necessary to properly level the varnish.

Tuesday, 19.

PERMANENT WOOD FILLING.—The letters P. W. F. are the initials of Permanent Wood Filling, a preparation designed as a priming over wood and iron, to take the place of lead-paint on carriages. *It fills the pores of the wood completely and permanently.* Being a liquid, it penetrates and fills every pore, and imparts to the wood a firm and superior surface for sustaining the coats of paint and varnish which follow. It is manufactured by Valentine & Company, 323

Pearl-street, and is sold in cans of one and five gallons capacity, at four dollars per gallon. It forms an important feature in the system known as "The American Method of Carriage-painting," which has been adopted by all the leading carriage-makers in this country, and many in France, Germany and England.

Wednesday, 20.

THAT only can be spoken of as a *work of art* which represents the beautiful and perfected thought of one master-mind. Many hands may assist in its realization, but the conception of the whole must be individual, and it must be one of beauty rather than one of mere utility.—*George Houghton.*

Thursday, 21.

THERE is a rule which never fails, and it reads as follows : The least paint applied to a body or gear, and have a smooth surface, the better. Close up the pores of the wood and under-coats of paint, and the brilliancy and fullness of the varnish will be ensured. It will require several applications of lead-paint to do the same amount of *filling*, or closing of the pores, as it will of P. W. F. The latter enters the pores and closes them at once, although to the casual observer it does not appear to do so. When once the pores are filled no further absorption will take place, and the varnish drying on the surface with its full complement of oil, will be far more durable than where a portion of the oil is absorbed.

Friday, 22.

CHIPPED WORK.—As a general thing, paint that is easily chipped from its foundation will not be improved by putting paint over it. However, we have seen work of that description done, with good results, as follows: Sandpaper down quite well with coarse sandpaper and lay on a coat of Permanent Wood Filling; let stand an hour to soak in, then wipe off with rags; give forty-eight hours to dry, and lay on elastic coats in subsequent painting. Japan brown or a black may be made by using Valentine's Black Japan (adding a little vermilion or Indian red for the brown). This being much more elastic than ordinary color, it tends to bind the chipping foundation of old paint, and will make an excellent job.

Saturday, 23.

VARNISH CHANGING COLOR.—Any finishing varnish, if exposed to a storm or even a heavy dew before it is thoroughly hardened, will turn white or *blue*. But when Valentine's Wearing Body or Elastic Gear is well dried before it is exposed to the elements, *it will not "bloom"* (the proper term for this deviltry), as experience has proved in many instances. The repeated blooming of varnish is highly detrimental to its lustre, even if its durability be not impaired, and a varnish that will *not* bloom should be the demand of a first-class workman.

Monday, 25.

THE following are a few of the maxims of Benjamin Franklin:

" Trade is the mother of money."

" Be beforehand with your business."

" Spend and be free, but make no waste."

" Credit is like a looking-glass—easily broken."

" Keep thy shop, and thy shop will keep thee."

" They never thrive who spend their time in beer-houses and in gaming-houses."

Tuesday, 26.

JAPAN GOLD-SIZE.—This is a dryer for paints, and is used in a similar manner to Brown Japan or Crown Coach Japan. It is *stronger and better* than Brown Japan, and one-half the quantity which is used of the latter will suffice to make the paint work nicely and to dry well. Too much Japan Gold-size added to the paint will make it saponaceous, or anti-drying. *It is not a sizing for gold*, and should never be used for that purpose. To make *Gilding-size*, take equal parts of Crown Coach Japan and Finishing Varnish, or one part Japan Gold-size and two parts P. W. F.

Wednesday, 27.

" ONE of the reasons why I have continued to improve may be reduced to a principle of honesty: I have endeavored *to do my best* if great or vulgar, good subjects or bad."

" Those who are determined to excel must go to their work whether willing or unwilling, morning, noon and night, and they will find it to be no play, but on the contrary very hard work."—*Sir Joshua Reynolds.*

Thursday, 28.

JAPAN BROWN.—A beautiful color, known by the above title. from the fact that Black Japan forms the principal ingredient, is used by carriage-painters, not only on account of its beauty, but because it is easily mixed and is a durable color. Various shades, from light to dark, may be made by simply changing the proportions of the two ingredients, namely, Valentine's Black Japan and red, either vermilion or Indian red. This paint, when properly mixed, is similar to color-and-varnish, and should be applied in a similar manner, *i. e.*, with varnish-brushes. It is excellent in repainting a carriage, in which case rub down the old varnish to remove gloss, and apply the Japan-brown directly to the work, two coats of which will generally make a very fair job.

Friday, 29.

ROUGHSTUFF.—Valentine's Ground Roughstuff may be thinned with turpentine if found too thick for use when taken from the original package. But this thinning must be done with judgment. We don't want to kill or injure the binding and elastic qualities of the mixture—we simply supply a little turpentine in the place of that which has evaporated. A small quantity of raw oil should be added when the roughstuff is intended for the first coat over P. W. F. (a tablespoonful to a pint of the roughstuff will be sufficient.)

Saturday, 30.

THE following definitions of rough-stuff are not to be found in any varnish-dealer's catalogue :

1. "*A coat of roughstuff*—A chinchilla ulster."—*The Hub.*

2. "Oh, no! Tar and feathers."—*Lynch County Gazette.*

3. "Oh, pshaw! Roughstuff? A dose of castor oil."—*Medical Times.*

4. "Roughstuff? One of Dennis Kearney's speeches."—*Greenback Bugle.*

5. "Roughstuff? Thyme and bread is a darned roughstuff for a poor turkey."—*Thanksgiving Times.*

1879 SEPT. 1879

"You may break, you may shatter the coach if you will,
But the paint we put it on will stick to it still."

Sun.	Mon.	Tue.	Wed.	Thu.	Fri.	Sat.
- -	1	2	3	4	5	6
7	8	9	10	11	12	13
14	15	16	17	18	19	20
21	22	23	24	25	26	27
28	29	30	- -	- -	- -	- -
- -	- -	- -	- -	- -	- -	- -

Monday, 1.

TRUE SENTIMENTS.

Let no mean jealousies pervert your mind,
A blemish in another's fame to find ;
Be grateful for the gifts that you possess,
Nor deem a rival's merits make yours less.

Tuesday, 2.

THE warm days are now followed by cold nights, and it is quite important that the heating arrangements of the varnish-room be attended to, and when varnished work is left to dry over night the temperature of the room be maintained at 70 or 75 degrees Fah. A change to a lower degree during the night would possibly cause "pitting," "going silky" or "sandy," and "crawling" of the varnish-coat.

SEPTEMBER, 1879.

Wednesday, 3.

WEIGHT OF LIQUIDS.—The following list shows the approximate weights of the different liquids used in coach-painting :

	Lbs.	Ozs.
1 pint of turpentine,		10
1 pint of linseed oil,	1	
1 pint of varnish,	1	
1 pint of Japan,	1	2
1 pint of roughstuff,	2	
1 pint of mixed black,	1	5
1 pint of lead-paint,	2	12

Thursday, 4.

RUBBING-COATS.—It is generally best to get a body or gear into color-and-varnish before applying clear rubbing-varnish, and this is done to *preserve the color* as well as to guard against pitting, crawling, etc., which is liable to occur where the clear varnish is laid over dead or "flat" color. This rule is not an arbitrary one, for many a good job is done with clear varnish, and this is especially the case where none but oily color (which would cause pitting of the varnish) is at hand for mixing the color-and-varnish.

Friday, 5.

A TRULY economical person will be as careful of his time as of his money. It is with the one as with the other—a few minutes here and a half hour there wasted on trifles, just as a few cents or dimes per day spent foolishly, will, in a short time, make a great loss, while on the other hand these fractions, whether of time or money, if economized, will, after a while, amount to a large capital.

Saturday, 6.

DARK RICH BROWN.—Take Indian red. five parts, and Prussian blue, one part ; grind and mix in Crown Coach Japan and turpentine ; add a very little oil. The color may be made light or dark, as desired, by simply altering the proportions. Vermilion and ivory black will make a very good brown, but we believe that all red and black browns are improved or softened in tone by the addition of yellow. Umber-brown, Vandyke-brown, sienna-brown, etc., are all pigments of the brown order, but require the addition of other pigments to lighten, darken, or to give them richness; as for example, umber-brown, without the addition of a drop or two of red, is a cold, raw color, unless placed in juxtaposition to the required reddish tint.

Monday, 8.
PAINTING SLEIGHS.

As soon as the woodwork is finished, give the outside of the sleigh a coat of Permanent Wood Filling and wipe off with rags, in the same manner as directed for carriage bodies. The inside, which is generally covered with canvas, should receive a coating of slush. There is in most shops a good supply of slush paint—the emptyings of cups and the settlings of varnish-cans. However, if you have none at hand, take any cheap pigment, such as mineral paint, Venetian red yellow ochre, etc.. and mix with oil and Japan.

Tuesday, 9.

The body of the sleigh requires roughstuff, and to-day, the P. W. F. being dry, apply an even coat of Valentine's Ground Roughstuff, bearing in mind that the better you keep the surface—that is, free from brush-marks, runs and dirt—the less labor you will have in all subsequent work. The running part may be puttied over the worst places, but do not attempt to thoroughly putty the holes, for the jarring given the wood by the smith will loosen the putty and make you double labor; simply glaze over the most open-grained places.

Wednesday, 10.

The second coat of roughstuff may be applied to the body to-day. Before laying it on, however, see that all nail and brad-holes are filled with putty. Late in the afternoon, if the job is a hurried one, the smith may take it to put on the irons. It is always best to have the ironing done while the job is in roughstuff, for not only does it give time for drying, but any injury the surface may receive while in the smith-shop may be easily repaired.

Thursday, 11.

In painting sleighs there is a much larger field for display than on carriages. They require to be painted with more showy colors and with more ornamentation, and the painter is called upon to choose from the variety of colors those suitable for this class of work, and to harmonize them, which is often a very trying task. In the vicinity of New York City and east of that place, the colors used on sleighs are generally dark, and but little ornamentation or striping is added; while in the North and West a more fanciful style is adopted. In our opinion the most cheerful colors should be chosen for sleighs, the dark shades for heavy work and the light ones for light work. A light cutter would look well with the panels bright vermilion, the armpiece and mouldings medium shade dark green, panels striped with double fine line of light green, and the armpiece with quarter-inch gold stripe edged with vermilion, and distanced with fine lines of canary yellow or a cream color. A monogram or ornament in center of dash panel inside, or on center of back panel. Full directions for painting a white sleigh will be found on another page.

Friday, 12.

The sleigh having returned from the smith-shop, look it over carefully and repair surface if needed. Then clean off running part with sandpaper and file, and give the wood and iron a coat of P. W. F. If the wings are to be covered with leather or canvas, coat the iron with P. W. F. to prevent rust.

Saturday, 13.

Put in to-day in rubbing the sleigh-body out of roughstuff and in smoothing the running part with sandpaper and putty, and cleaning the whole job for color. Lay all color on with a camel's-hair brush, to ensure smoothness, and besides this kind of brush is economical, for it saves color by laying it thinner. The color should be mixed to dry with an egg-shell gloss, not too dead nor too glossy.

Monday, 15.

Two coats of color may be necessary, and if so, the second coat may be put on this morning; if not, apply a coat of color-and-varnish to all parts. If it is necessary to apply the second coat of color, the color-and-varnish may be put on late in the afternoon. Mix the color in Valentine's Elastic Leveling Varnish for body, and in Quick Leveling Varnish for the running part. Apply "full," and as clean as if it was for the finish.

Tuesday, 16.

There is oftentimes trouble with striping where gold-bronze is substituted for gold-leaf, but the remedy for the trouble lies in the hands of the painter. If the bronze is of poor quality, it will be found coarse and will not adhere well to the size. If put on to size that is not sufficiently "tacky," it will be drowned and turn green, whether of good or bad quality. If the size be too dry the bronze will not adhere to it. The *best* bronze should therefore be purchased in all cases, and the size carefully watched to see when the "tack" is just right.

Wednesday, 17.

A light rub with pumice-stone and water will prepare the job for the striper and ornamenter. If gold is to be put on, it will be necessary to prepare the surface so that the leaf or bronze will adhere to no part but that covered by size, and to do this we pounce the parts to be gilded with a pounce-bag, made by tying some whiting in muslin to form a bag. A thin film of whiting is thus put on, and the application of the gilding-size next follows.

Thursday, 18.

The striping, etc., being finished, wash the job off with clean water, chamois dry, and run it into the varnish-room, where it may receive a good coat of Quick Leveling or Elastic Leveling varnish as a rubbing-coat over the striping ; for if but one coat of finishing varnish is put on we fear it would not make as good a job as we desire.

Friday, 19.

Decalcomanie pictures, or "transfers," are a ready means of ornamenting, and these are used by many sleigh-builders in the country.

But the scroll patterns designed for such work, and often illustrated in *The Hub*, if well executed by hand, give better satisfaction to the customer, as well as value to the work, and show that care was expended in the production of the job; whereas with the transfers a *cheap* appearance is given.

Saturday, 20.

The trimmer may now call for the job to put in linings, etc., and as it is quite dry we send it off to be trimmed, which will take a day, perhaps. All this time the rubbing-coat is hardening, and when we next apply the rub-rag we will find that a smooth surface is easily obtained. A woolen rag is best for use as a rub-rag, although some prefer felt. The main thing is to have your rubbing-coats so clean and well laid that but little rubbing is necessary. *There is no earthly use of putting on varnish and then rubbing it half off.*

Monday, 22.

COLOR FOR SLEIGHS.—The most fashionable colors used in the Eastern States are: Black striped with gold; black body striped with light cream color, with lake or carmine runners; carmine striped with gold and black; pea-green striped with gold and black; or lake striped with gold and vermilion, in connection with black or vermilion runners. A pure white sleigh, or white striped with vermilion, is sometimes called for; while some customers prefer the entire sleigh in black without striping. Any colors that harmonize together can be used on sleigh work without infringing on good taste.

Tuesday, 23.

To-day is the finishing day of the sleigh. Being nicely rubbed and washed, flow on every part a coat of Valentine's Medium Drying Body Varnish, and the job is done.

Wednesday, 24.

WORK is, as a rule, at the foundation of all true success. Brilliant parts, fine education, powerful friends, are not to be despised, but they cannot supply the place of personal toil and patient pains-taking industry. President Lincoln literally worked himself up from a common laborer to the highest position in the gift of the Republic. Henry Wilson, at twenty-one, carried his wardrobe and his library on his back whithersoever he went in pursuit of work. Commodore Vanderbilt laid the foundation of his vast fortune in the savings and habits of industry acquired in his young days in rowing a ferry-boat. Charles Dickens owed his success not more to his genius than to hard, systematic labor. "Industry is the sheet-anchor of success."

Thursday, 25.

TO MIX TINTS.—Tints are colors added to white, and to mix them the white-lead should first be thinned to a cream-like consistency with turpentine, and the staining ingredient—that is, any desired color—should be mixed in a similar manner in a separate vessel. Then add the stain little by little to the white until the tint required is obtained. It must be remembered that some pigments are very strong, and the least drop will change the tint, while other pigments, being weak, will occasion the use of quite a large percentage. Experience will prove the best teacher in this matter.

Friday, 26.

THE *Technologist* says that the so-called lead-paralysis, common among painters in the form of a loss of motion of the wrist-joints, is chiefly produced by the habit of washing the hands in turpentine. It is probable that it is not the turpentine alone which produces this fatal result, but chiefly the particles of lead or zinc-paint on the hands, which, by the turpentine, are brought in a condition to penetrate the skin more readily and to be absorbed. Therefore, painters should avoid, as much as possible, the use of turpentine for washing the hands, and the use of white lead in their work.

Saturday, 27.

ARTIFICIAL CORAL.—Melt together yellow resin, four parts; vermilion, one part. This gives a very pretty effect to glass, twigs, raisin-stems, cinders, stones, etc., dipped into the mixture and dried.

Monday, 29.

THERE are times when a heaviness comes over the heart, and we feel as if there was no hope. Who has not felt it? For this there is no cure but work. Plunge into it; put all your energies into motion; rouse up the inner man. Act, and this heaviness shall disappear as mist before the morning sun. Work, then, and faint not; for therein is the well-spring of human hope and human happiness.—*Cassius M. Clay.*

Tuesday, 30.

PAINTING OLD WORK.—To repaint a badly-chipped gear, first scrape off all the old paint, and this may be easily done with a well-ground flat file. Take a twelve or fourteen-inch flat file that has been "used up" in the smith-shop, and grind the two sides and the edges sufficient to make four sharp, square corners, and you will have an excellent scraping tool. After scraping, finish well with coarse sandpaper, dust off, and apply a coat of P. W. F.; wipe off well with clean rags, and give forty-eight hours for drying. Then proceed as you would with the painting. Providing the paint is not in bad condition *all over* the gear, those parts which are chipped the most may be scraped, and the other parts simply sandpapered over. The coating of P. W. F. over all will furnish a good foundation for subsequent painting.

GENERAL SYNOPSIS OF THE AMERICAN METHOD FOR SLEIGHS.

1st day,	Coat P. W. F. all over.	give 24 hours, if well wiped.	
2d "	1st coat roughstuff, .	give 48 hours.	
4th "	2d " " ordinary, .	" 24 "	
5th "	Rub body, sandpaper runners, and putty same.		
6th "	Color all over, . .	give 16 hours.	
6th "	2d coat of color all over,	" 18 "	
7th "	Color and varnish all over,	" 24 "	
8th "	Stripe and ornament.		
9th "	Rubbing varnish all over, .	" 24 "	
10th	Finish with Medium Drying Varnish.		

1879 OCTOBER. 1879

*" Buy the best that you can buy,
Mix well and give time to dry."*

Sun.	Mon.	Tue.	Wed.	Thu.	Fri.	Sat.
- -	- -	- -	1	2	3	4
5	6	7	8	9	10	11
12	13	14	15	16	17	18
19	20	21	22	23	24	25
26	27	28	29	30	31	- -
- -	- -	- -	- -	- -	- -	- -

Wednesday, 1.

BE CAREFUL WHAT YOU SAY.

In speaking of a person's faults,
Pray don't forget your own ;
Remember, those with homes of glass
Should seldom throw a stone :
If we have nothing else to do
Than talk of those who sin,
'Tis better to commence at home,
And from that point begin.

Thursday, 2.

THIS month the painter will, no doubt, be annoyed with the deviltry known as "going sandy," "seedy," and "specky," in the varnish-room. This is a trouble brought about by the varnish being *chilled*, and may be prevented by keeping the cans of varnish in a warm place at all times; and by thoroughly warming the varnish that has been chilled, it may return to its proper condition and give good results when spread upon the work. Varnish is frequently chilled while in transit from the manufactory to the paint-shop, but most frequently by the practice of setting the varnish-cans upon the floor (the coldest part of the shop).

Friday, 3.

COLOR-AND-VARNISH.—When about to make color-and-varnish, the painter should be careful not to use *oily* color, for the varnish will not readily assimilate with oil, and the consequence is that the deviltries known as silking, pitting and crawling will appear in the coating before it becomes dry. Color-and-varnish should be made by mixing quick color with the varnish, or better still, to mix the dry pigment with the varnish, and grind it through the mill. Where several pigments are employed to form a color this cannot be done so well, and in that case use quick, or japan color, oil color never.

Saturday, 4.

It is invariably the case that people who have had a small estate left them, which they know not the getting of, think "It is day, and will never be night;" that a little to be spent out of so much, is not worth minding. A child and fool, as Poor Richard says, imagine twenty shillings and twenty years can never be spent; but always be taking out of the meal-tub, and never putting in, soon comes to the bottom; then when the well is dry, they know the worth of water.

Monday, 6.

GILDING SIZE.—Take Valentine's finishing varnish and add an equal portion of Crown Coach Japan, or a little less Japan Gold Size, whichever is at hand; or take equal parts Permanent Wood Filling (light shade) and C. C. Japan; mix with either of the above a little chrome yellow to give the requisite thickness on body, and to aid in drawing straight stripes. Now, being all prepared, draw the stripes directly upon the prepared surface the same as if it were paint that was in use instead of gilding-size. When the stripes have been on, say one hour, feel with the finger if the *size* is "tacky;" if not wait a while until it is so ; then lift one of the paper-leaves, with the gold adhering, and lay it, with the gold down, upon the *size ;* rub over the whole gently with the finger and lift the paper, when it will be found that the gold leaf is firmly affixed to the stripe. Proceed in the same manner until all the *size* is covered with gold ; after which give time for drying, and wash off with clean water.

Tuesday, 7.

ONCE begun a thing is almost half-finished.

HE who thinks for himself, and imitates rarely, is a free man.

OLD and young men should pattern after pianos—be square, upright and grand.

WRITE me down az one who fears God, luvs to ketch trout, pla whist, and ride a three minnitt gait.

Wednesday, 8.

HOW TO KEEP PAINT BRUSHES.—All brushes used for painting should be suspended in water to prevent the paint from drying in the hair or bristles. This is best done by making a hole in the handle, through which to run a wire, then placing the brush and wire in position, allowing the ends of the wire to rest on the edge of the vessel, and being careful to have just water enough to reach up to the binding ; for if it be allowed to cover it there is a liability of injuring the brush by swelling the handle and bursting the cord. Turpentine may be a very good liquid in which to suspend soft-hair pencils, temporarily, but it soon rots the hair and ruins the brush. Varnish-brushes should be suspended in varnish—*nothing else.*

Thursday, 9.

HOW TO GET ALONG IN THE WORLD.—If you have a place of business, be found there when wanted. No man can get rich by sitting around stores and saloons.

Never fool in business matters.

Have order, system, regularity, and also promptness.

Do not meddle with business you know nothing about.

Do not kick every one in your path.

More miles can be made in one day by going steadily than by stopping.

Pay as you go.

A man of honor respects his word as he does his bond.

Help others when you can, but never give what you cannot afford because it is fashionable.

Learn to say No. No necessity of snapping it out dog-fashion, but say it firmly and respectfully.

Use your own brains rather than those of others.

Learn to think and act for yourself.

Keep ahead rather than behind the times.

Friday, 10.

OILING WORK.—We would say that the custom of rubbing jobs with oil while in the repository is not common, though we understand that it has been tried by a number of carriage-builders in various parts of the country. Pure olive oil, if rubbed over the varnish surface of a carriage, when considerably deadened by use or by storage in an ill-ventilated repository, would brighten it to some extent; but, on the contrary, if applied to jobs newly varnished, it would deaden their lustre. The only way to bring back the lustre to new work is to wash it often with cold water, and each washing will tend to harden and improve the varnish.

Saturday, 11.

"CAPTAIN," said a son of Erin, as a ship was nearing the coast in inclement weather, "have ye a almenik on board?" "No, I haven't." "Then, be jabers, we shall have to take the weather as it comes."

"Pay me that six-and-eight-pence you owe me, Mr. Malrooney," said a village attorney. "For what?" "For the opinion you had of me." "Faith, I never had any opinion of you in all my life."

HE wouldn't swear to it.—A witness, on entering the box, had a testament presented to him, but he declined to be sworn. Being asked his reasons for refusing, he naively replied: "I'll tell a lie w' ony mon i' England, but I'll not swear to it."

OCTOBER, 1879.

Monday, 13.

CHAMOIS-SKIN.—The skin used by the painter for drying off water, and called a "shammy," derives its name from the chamois, an animal of the antelope kind, whose hide was, and may occasionally be still in use; but we are seldom fortunate enough to secure a *real* chamois-skin, those sold for such being generally only alum-dressed sheep-skins. The best are thin, though compact and soft, and generally a lighter color than the poorer qualities. Care should be taken to keep them free from dirt, grease, soap, etc., which would tend to injure the work. Never use a chamois for drying the hands and face when washing.

Tuesday, 14.

JUDGING BY FACES.—A man's character is stamped upon his face by the time that he is thirty. I had rather put my trust in any human being's countenance than his words. The lips may lie, the face can not. To be sure, " a man may smile and smile and be a villain ;" but what a smile it is—a false widening of the mouth and increasing of the cheeks, an unpleasant grimace that makes the observer shudder. "Rascal" is legibly written all over it.

Wednesday, 15.

PERMANENT WOOD FILLING makes an excellent oil finish on most woods. But rosewood, which is excessively oily, it will not penetrate, and therefore shellac is best. Upon Georgia pine care must be taken to wipe it well with rags, that the close, sappy places be not overcharged with it.

Thursday, 16.

I DON'T kno whitch feels the biggest, the nuly elekted sheriff ov one ov the rural countys, or the man who drives four-in-hand for the fust time.

ENNY man who kan swop horses, or ketch fish, and not lie about it, is just about az pious az men ever get to be in this world.

THE shortest way to a woman's harte iz to praze her baby and her bonnet ; and to a man's harte, to praze his watch and his horse and buggy.

IT takes a live man to do bizziness now-a-days. I don't care if you hav got a copy ov the Bible to sell, you hav got to talk it up strong.

Friday, 17.

HOW TO DEVISE A NEW COLOR.—When the painter goes to the stone to mix a new color, he will find it a good plan—providing he does not have before him a sample of the desired color—to first gaze a little while into vacancy, as it is called—that is, to look intently at a blank wall without directing the mind at the thing gazed upon, and at the same time to conjure up in his "mind's eye" the color he wishes to produce. This proceeding may appear a waste of time to some, but those who have practiced it will understand its utility in bringing the eye to a proper condition to judge correctly concerning any combination of pigments which at the time is under preparation.

The painter sees in his mind's eye, for example, a brilliant orange color, and he then turns out yellow and red, and works them together until the eye is satisfied. A lighter or darker tint than the one first imagined can then be quickly discovered, and the proportions altered until the desired hue is obtained.

This method of arriving at conclusions as regards color was first taught us by our "old boss" many years ago, while we were yet in our teens, and we cheerfully endorse the method as one which has served us well in the years gone by. Try it, reader, and write us your opinion.

Saturday, 18.

I don't care if yu have got a hed full ov branes, and a harte full ov honesty, if yu kant git yure note diskounted for 60 days, yu ain't mutch ov a phellow for theze times.

After a day's weary march Mohammed was camping with his followers. One said, "I will loose my camel and commit it to God." Mohammed said, "Friend, tie thy camel, and commit it to God."

When a poor little blind boy was asked what forgiveness is, he paused a moment, and then, taking his pen, wrote: "It is the odor which the trampled flower gives out to bless the foot which crushed it."

Monday, 20.

RUBBING.—In rubbing the body be careful that the pumice-stone does not *dry* on the surface. Keep it well wet, until washed from the job. After the first rubbing and washing, rub it again lightly with pulverized rotten-stone and water; then wash clean, using a water-tool (a painter's sash-tool) to remove dirt from corners of moldings, etc.; then, having a good chamois-skin (not a common sheep-skin), dry the work thoroughly, and there will be no "motes" to remove. When ready to apply the varnish, put a little varnish in the hollow of the hand and gently moisten the ends of the bristles of the duster; this attracts any fine lint that may be on the panel, and a very light dusting over will give you as clean a job as you could have. Rubbing the hand over a panel is apt to cause trouble from the perspiration left upon it. The finishing strokes in varnishing should be up and down, excepting on narrow and long horizontal parts. And all varnish should be left to *flow* before it begins to *set*.

Tuesday, 21.

SOME people have expressed themselves as discouraged in their expectation of finding any art in America, and have "long ceased to hope!" Let us remember that art, like jelly, has always been more easily recognized when cold. It has always existed, in all nations, and the tradition will probably not die here. Art is not always recognized in the present. In fact, most people prefer it *canned!*

Wednesday, 22.

JAPAN GOLD SIZE.—The name Japan Gold Size has ever been a source of misunderstanding to painters, and we are not surprised at your question. It is not adapted for use as a *gilding size*, but it forms an important ingredient in making gilding size, as will be seen by the following formula: Take of Permanent Wood Filling one part, Japan Gold Size one part, mix well and apply; this size, if laid on thin, will be ready for gilding in about twelve hours. The length of time between laying on the size and the application of the gold should be regulated by the proportion of the ingredients used; the more P. W. F., the longer the time required for drying; the more Japan Gold Size, the shorter the time; the latter alone does not possess binding or "sticking" properties sufficient to hold or fasten the gold leaf. Any high grade finishing varnish, tempered with Japan Gold Size as a dryer, will make a good *gilding size*.

Thursday, 23.

A FINE imitation of ebony, and one that is really better for service than the wood itself, is made from pear, beech, maple, or any close-grained wood. Boil the chips of logwood in an iron vessel, and saturate the wood to be dyed several times until the liquid penetrates the grain ; then take iron fillings, or rusty iron, and pour vinegar over it. Let it remain until done effervescing, and then apply it to the wood while wet with the logwood juice. This will make a fine ebony black, and will admit of sandpapering and polishing equal to the natural wood.

Friday, 24.

P. W. F.—Permanent Wood Filling will be found excellent in closing up the porosity of brick, and thereby preventing the absorption of the oil from the paint put on over it, and you will find that one good coat of paint will be quite sufficient to give a finish, when applied over the P. W. F., where two coats are generally necessary. It is calculated, that one gallon of P. W. F. will cover eight hundred square feet of surface on wood, but we think that the brick-work will drink up a little more, and we might set it down as six hundred square feet for a gallon. By the use of P. W. F. on brown stone fronts, the color of the stone will be improved, and as it is impossible for dampness to penetrate through it, the serious trouble of frost-cracks, and chipping of the stone will be wholly avoided.

Saturday, 25.

We are apt to put off the great work until a time of leisure ; but, believe me, no masterpiece of human industry or ingenuity was ever so accomplished. The vacation comes ; we loll on the bridge, whistle, or drop pebbles into the running water, but the very thought of a great project becomes wearisome.—*Geo. Houghton.*

Monday, 27.

AMERICAN VERMILION is inferior, as a general thing, to the English, but one brand, called California vermilion, is a beautiful color, and not so liable to darken as other American vermilion. The ordinary American vermilion is used extensively on trucks and farm wagons, and for such work it answers the purpose very well, but for fine work we prefer the English.

Tuesday, 28.

It is not work that kills men ; it is worry. Work is healthy. You can hardly put more work upon a man than he can bear. Worry is rust upon the blade. It is not the resolution that destroys the machinery, but the friction.

Wednesday, 29.

ULTRAMARINE.—When this pigment is used as a glazing over a blue ground, it should be ground in hard-drying body varnish, and thinned with very little turpentine when about to be applied. When it is to be used as a color—without glazing, save as color-and-varnish—mix with Japan Gold Size and turpentine to grind, then add a few drops of oil—testing it upon the thumb-nail until it dries with an egg-shell gloss—to make it elastic and durable.

Thursday, 30.

You may talk as much as you please about man being able to accomplish anything he undertakes if he sets about it in earnest—we demur. When it comes to scratching the back dead square between the shoulders, a fat man has to let out the job. He may pierce the ocean wave with the lightning's flash, make fraud an honored profession, get up a telephone that will carry Russian names without bending the wire, but he comes to an impassable stone fence sometimes.

Friday, 31.

BADLY-CHIPPED PAINT.—To repaint a badly-chipped gear, first scrape off all the old paint, and this may be easily done with a well-ground flat file. Take a twelve or fourteen inch flat file that has been "used up" in the smith-shop, and grind the sides and edges sufficient to make four sharp, square corners, and you will have an excellent scraping tool. After scraping. finish with coarse sandpaper (No. $3\frac{1}{2}$), dust off and apply a coat of P. W. F., wipe off well, and then proceed in the usual manner of painting by the American Method. If the paint is not badly chipped (simply cracked), sandpaper down well to remove as much of the outside shell of varnish as possible, then apply P. W. F., and go on as if dealing with a new gear.

Have you not heard of the man who made two holes in his fence for his cats to crawl through—one large, for grown cats, and one small, for kittens? If so, you will readily preceive the similarity between that man and the painter who puts one or more coats of lead-paint over a priming of P. W. F.

1879 NOV. 1879

*"He who paints to please his master,
Must paint, not only well, but faster."*

Sun.	Mon.	Tue.	Wed.	Thu.	Fri.	Sat.
--	--	--	--	--	--	1
2	3	4	5	6	7	8
9	10	11	12	13	14	15
16	17	18	19	20	21	22
23	24	25	26	27	28	29
30	--	--	--	--	--	--

Saturday, 1.

OUR FAULTS.

We have no right to judge a man
  Until he's fairly tried ;
Should we not like his company,
  We know the world is wide.
Some may have faults—and who has not?
  The old as well as young ;
Perhaps we may, for aught we know,
  Have fifty to their one.

Monday, 3.

THE nights being cold at this time, and heavy dews or frosts of frequent occurrence in some sections, it will be necessary to run all work from the drying-sheds into the shop at night, otherwise the outer shell or coating of paint will be *chilled hard*, and being apparently dry the painter may be led into the error of applying the next coat too soon.

Tuesday, 4.

SWEATING OF VARNISH.—Varnish will "sweat," that is, have a glossy appearance after it has been rubbed and allowed to stand a while, if the coat has been applied too heavy, and has not dried through. If too much rubbing is done, the rubbing coat is too often applied carelessly, with the thought that all defects, such as specks and brush-marks, will be rubbed out, but this necessitates so long a rubbing that the "life" of the varnish is rubbed out, and sweating follows as a natural consequence. However, sweating is of no consequence in the hands of an experienced workman, for he will rub the job and put the varnish on before it has time to sweat.

Wednesday, 5.

LORD CHESTERFIELD was dining at an inn where the plates were dirty. Lord C., complaining, was informed by the waiter that "every one must eat a peck of dirt before he dies." "That may be true," said Chesterfield, "but no one is obliged to eat it all at one meal."

Thursday, 6.

CLEANING VARNISH BRUSHES.—It is true that turpentine is bad for a brush, and to clean a good brush it should never be slopped into a cup of turpentine. Ordinarily it can best be cleaned by working the dust out on some unimportant panel. If the brush has become dirty by an unlucky fall to the floor, hold it at an angle towards the floor, in such a manner that when the turpentine is poured upon it, the spirits will not run up into the hilt of the brush, but will flow off, carrying with it the greater part of the dirt. After rinsing it in this manner, strike the tin binding several sharp raps upon some hard substance, when the recoil or spring of the hair will cleanse the brush of the turpentine. Rinse well in rubbing varnish and work it out nicely on an old panel.

Friday, 7.

HOT WATER.—It is the habit of some painters, as well as stablemen, to use hot water for washing a job, during cold weather; and we have known some to use it even in rubbing varnish or roughstuff; and we take this opportunity to warn all such against such a proceeding. Hot water not only softens the surface of paint or varnish, but penetrates deeply into a roughstuff surface, causing trouble in subsequent coats, or delay by its slow evaporation.

Water from which the *chill* is removed only, is the requirement. *Hot water*, never!

Saturday, 8.

MIXING VARNISHES.—Valentine's varnishes may be mixed together to suit the requirements of certain cases without detriment, as for example: If you are using Elastic Gear varnish, and the job is a hurried one, and the day damp or rainy, add a little Quick Leveling Varnish and stir well together, this will cause it to dry well. For Wearing Body add a little Hard Drying Varnish. This feature of mixing this brand of varnishes is a good one, and often of service to the painter, but he must use judgment, for the responsibility all rests with him, and his care must be not to add *too much* of the lower grade varnish, and thereby injure the durability of the work. A *little* will do no harm.

Monday, 10.

Don't stand sighing, wishing and waiting, but go to work with an energy and perseverance that will set every object in the way of success flying like leaves before a whirlwind. A milk-and-water way of doing business leaves a man in the lurch every time. He may have ambition enough to wish himself on the topmost round of the ladder of success, but if he has not got the go-aheaditiveness to pull himself up there, he will inevitably remain at the bottom, or at best, on the very low rounds.

Tuesday, 11.

VARNISH BRUSHES.—The flat bristle brush if well made, and of the proper shape, size and quality of stock is best for general varnishing on bodies—and many prefer them also on gears. A set of the New-York Standard varnish brushes, made by Miles Bros., of Fulton-st., from one-half an inch to three inches in width, will be found excellent tools: the cost of these are $3.50 per set. Fitch-hair brushes are used to some extent, but the badger-hair brush is its superior in every respect.

Wednesday, 12.

VARNISHING GOLD BRONZE.—It may have been noticed by the painter that English varnishes invariably cause a speedy darkening or greening of the metal, owing no doubt to an acid present in the varnish which draws the verdigris to the surface, while this is not the case with American varnishes; and we advise the use of a rubbing coat of American varnish where English varnish *must* be used over gold. Valentine's Finishing Varnishes do not affect the color of gold and may be used with perfect safety.

Thursday, 13.

MEN should not think too much of themselves, and yet a man should be careful not to forget himself.—*Prentice.*

THE more enlarged is our mind, the more we discover in men of originality. Your commonplace people see no difference between one and another.—*Pascal.*

A CHINESE lawyer has been admitted to the London bar. He will, no doubt, be able to Chin-esely enough, when the proper time comes.

Friday, 14.

FINISHING VARNISH.—The troubles called "crawling," "running," and working "tough" in a coat of finishing varnish are caused frequently by

1. Cold weather, cold room, cold varnish, or cold panels.
2. Greasy or dirty sponges or chamois.
3. A sweated under-coat.
4. Perspiration from the hands after the rubbing is done.
5. Brushes kept suspended in oil or turpentine.
6. A surface of English finishing varnish rubbed for another coat.

Saturday, 15.

THERE are some things for doing which one will not repent, viz.:
For hearing before judging;
For thinking before speaking:
For holding an angry tongue;
For stopping the ear to tale-bearers;
For disbelieving most floating gossip;
For refusing to kick a fallen man;
For being kind to the distressed;
For being patient toward everybody;
For doing good as he has opportunity;
For asking pardon for wrongs and mistakes;
For speaking evil of no one;
For being polite to all.

NOVEMBER, 1879.

Monday, 17.

KEEPING VARNISH BRUSHES.—Keep your varnish brushes suspended in the same kind of varnish you intend to use them in, and *never* in oil or turpentine. The least admixture of oil to a high-grade —that is, best quality—varnish will be apt to cause trouble, and by keeping your brushes in varnish you will find them ever ready for use.

Tuesday, 18.

VARNISHING IN SUMMER.—Having brought the work up to the leveling varnish coats and produced a smooth, even surface for the application of the finishing varnish, the surface must be rubbed with fine pumice-stone and water, well washed with cold water, and the varnish applied as *promptly as possible*, otherwise the surface is liable to "sweat" and give trouble. The varnish-room should be well ventilated, either by ventilators in the windows or by a pipe running through the ceiling and roof, or the amount of oxygen in the room will be insufficient to *harden* the varnish.

Wednesday, 19.

MARK TWAIN says "he has a higher standard of principle than George Washington. Washington couldn't tell a lie. He can, but he won't."

A MAN looking at the picture of a pig, inquired: "Who is that pigment for?"

Thursday, 20.

RUBBING-CLOTHS.—In rubbing bodies with pulverized pumice-stone, some prefer a piece of thick felt, others a piece of an old felt hat, but we prefer *woolen cloth*. Have one or two thicknesses drawn over a block of wood for rubbing large panels, and then finish up with a piece which can be folded to suit the shape of the work. The refuse pieces of the trimming-shop are best; old trimming is apt to be filled with grit or with tacks, which might injure the work by scratching it.

Friday, 21.

IF you have a friend who loves you, who has studied your interest and happiness, defended you when persecuted and troubled, be sure to sustain him in his adversity.

Saturday, 22.

PER-CENTAGES IN MIXING.—The painter is told at times to mix certain articles in the proportion of 5 per cent., or 10 per cent., etc., and we have often been asked by workmen to more clearly define the amount indicated by these figures. Five per cent. means simply five parts out of one hundred. If we are told to add 5 per cent. of oil to a quantity of paint, we must first calculate the amount of paint we have: supposing we are to make 20 gills of color, or 5 pints, then 1 gill would be 1 part of 20, or 5 parts in 100, which would be 5 per cent. Therefore, 1 gill in 20 gills, or 1 pound in 20 pounds would be 5 per cent. Ten per cent. is 10 parts in 100, and means, consequently, as above shown, 2 gills in 20 gills, or 1 gill in 10 gills.

Monday, 24.

JOHNNIE lost his knife. After searching in one pocket and another until he had been through all without success, he exclaimed: "Oh, dear! I wish I had another pocket, it might be in that!"

A VISITOR at an art gallery being asked whether he preferred pictures to statuary, said he preferred the latter, as "you kin go all around the statoos, but you can't see only one side of the picters."

Tuesday, 25.

STAINING OAK GRAINING.—If it be desired to change a piece of oak-grained work, as in house painting, to a black-walnut color, take enameled leather dressing, and apply an even coating over the oak grain, which will stain it a beautiful black-walnut color, and require no further operations, for the dressing acts as a stain and a varnish at the same time. In staining black-walnut, or any dark-colored woods, to mahogany color, put half an ounce of dragon's blood with two ounces of good alcohol, and shake occasionally; when dissolved, put as much of this stain into alcohol as will make the wood the color desired, and go over with a brush. For light-colored woods, such as pine, beach, etc., add a little burnt umber to the above stain. To stain rosewood, apply to any light-colored wood a coat of asphaltum thinned with turpentine, and when dry, stain with dragon's blood—but there will be no rosewood grain—merely the color.

NOVEMBER, 1879.

Wednesday, 26.

CONSCIENCE is your magnetic needle. Reason is your chart. But I would rather have a crew willing to follow the indications of the needle, and giving themselves no great trouble as to the chart, than a crew that had ever so good a chart and no needle at all.—*Joseph Cook.*

Thursday, 27.

THE impracticability of effectually concealing the cracks in a painted surface by the application of putty or paint has been fully demonstrated by many of the best carriage-painters in the country, and yet there are those who believe that they can do such work successfully. There have been several " crack-fillers " or roughstuffs put in the market which it was said would fill up the old cracks in a carriage-body so that they would not again appear, but we have yet to see a job done with any of these nostrums that will not show the old cracks in time. The best method of repainting where scraping or burning off is impracticable is, to sandpaper or rub the old surface well, then apply P. W. F., and proceed in the same manner as if it was a *new* job.

Friday, 28.

LITTLE THINGS.—There are a thousand and one little things connected with the painting business that are seldom, if ever, spoken of, or even thought of, by the majority of painters ; while, if a person will take trouble to examine closely, he will find that it is these little things that go to make up our first-class finished jobs. The painter who overlooks them will turn out work with a superficial finish ; it won't bear close inspection ; and he wonders why it is that his work is inferior to that of the workman across the street.

Saturday, 29.

DESTROY YOUR ENEMIES.—It is recorded of a Chinese Emperor, that on being told that his enemies had revolted in one of the distant provinces, he said to his officers : " Come, follow me, and we will quickly *destroy* them. He marched forward, and the rebels submitted at his approach.

All now thought that he would take revenge, and were surprised to see the captives treated with kindness and humanity. " How ! " said the chief officer, "is this the manner in which your majesty fulfills your promise? Your royal word was given that your enemies should be destroyed, and behold, you have pardoned them all, and even caressed some of them!" "I promised," replied the emperor, "to destroy my enemies, and have fulfilled my word, for see, they are *enemies* no longer; I have made *friends* of them."

The cleanliness and cheerful aspect of the paint-shop may be improved by a few *little things*. The paint-mill, the cans, tubs, boxes, etc., that are used around the paint-bench may be coated frequently (some Saturday night) with cheap or waste color—a dark green, for example, made with yellow and black; this will brighten up the bench, and the painter will begin his weekly toil cheerfully.

Homely Maxims.—Take care of your pennies.

Look well to your spending.

No matter what comes in, if more goes out you will always be poor.

The art is not in making money, but in keeping it.

Little expenses, like mice in a barn, when they are many, make a great waste.

Hair by hair heads get bald; straw by straw the thatch goes off the cottage, and drop by drop the rain comes into the chamber.

A barrel is soon empty if the tap leaks but a drop a minute.

When you mean to save, begin with your mouth; many thieves pass down the red lane.

The ale jug is a great waste.

In all other things keep within compass.

Never stretch your legs further than your blanket will reach, or you will soon be cold.

In clothes choose suitable and lasting stuff, and not tawdry fineries.

To be warm is the main thing; never mind the looks.

A fool may make money, but it needs a wise man to spend it.

Remember it is easier to build two chimneys than to keep one going.

If you give all to the back and board there is nothing left for the savings bank.

Fare hard and work hard when you are young, and you will have a chance to rest when you are old.

1879 DEC. 1879

"IF well you weigh it you'll decide
That paint, to stand, must be well dried."

Sun.	Mon.	Tue.	Wed.	Thu.	Fri.	Sat.
- -	1	2	3	4	5	6
7	8	9	10	11	12	13
14	15	16	17	18	19	20
21	22	23	24	25	26	27
28	29	30	- -	- -	- -	- -
- -	- -	- -	- -	- -	- -	- -

Monday, 1.

DEAL FAIRLY.

Ne'er labor for an idle boast
   Of victory o'er another ;
But while you strive your uttermost,
   Deal fairly with a brother.
Choose well the path in which you run—
   Succeed by noble daring ;
Then, though the last, when once 'tis won,
   Your crown is worth the wearing.

Tuesday, 2.

THE deviltries which are most likely to occur this month, are pitting, crawling, silking, streaking, etc., and these are almost in every case attributable to cold. The temperature of the varnish-room should be maintained at not less than 70 degrees Fahrenheit.

Wednesday, 3.

A LOCOMOTIVE engineer, who had just been discharged for some cause, gave vent to his spite in a way eminently characteristic of American humor. He said it was about time he left the company anyhow, for the sake of his life, for "there was nothing left of the track but two streaks of rust and the right of way."

Thursday, 4.

RE-PAINTING.—One of the best plans we know of for re-painting over an old, cracked job, is to rub down the body with lump pumice-stone, wash off and let dry; then put on a coat of Permanent Wood Filling in the same manner as if priming a job. When dry, glaze over the largest cracks with soft putty, to which has been added a little pulverized pumice-stone, let dry, and apply one or two coats of rough-stuff. When the latter is dry, rub down to a smooth surface, and proceed with the coloring in the usual way. This plan will close up or hide the cracks for a long time, but they *will show* again, and *nothing* can prevent it.

Friday, 5.

"WHAT a dignity it gives an old lady, that balance at the banker's! How tenderly we look at her faults if she is a relative. What a kind, good-natured, old creature we find her."—*Thackeray.*

"HE that wants money, means and content, is without three good friends."—*Shakespeare.*

Saturday, 6.

PRUSSIAN BLUE.—The best method of mixing this pigment to form a natural color, or its tints with white, is to pulverize and mix to a stiff paste with Crown Coach Japan, then grind in the mill, and add a very little raw oil. To form light blue tints, add the blue, drop by drop (it is very strong), to white paint until the shade desired is produced.

DECEMBER, 1879.

Monday, 8.
PAINTING CHEAP WORK.

SUPPOSING the job to be a buggy, first coat the body, beds, bars, wheels, reaches, etc., of the gears with Permanent Wood Filling, and wipe off with clean rags. The gear wood-work may then be sent to the smith-shop, but the body should remain in paint-shop, and be kept either in a warm room or in the sun and air.

Tuesday, 9.

APPLY a coat of Valentine's Ground Roughstuff, having about five per cent. of raw oil added, to the body, laying it on as smoothly as possible, and being careful that the roughstuff is not too thick, else brush-marks will be liable to show in the finish. No matter how well the job may be rubbed and painted over an uneven coat of roughstuff, the rough or streaked coating will be plainly seen in the finish.

Wednesday, 10.

PUTTY up all imperfections in the body, this morning, and late this afternoon the second coat of roughstuff may be applied. The putty used for this job may be made by a mixture of one part rubbing varnish, one part Crown Coach Japan, thickened to the proper consistency of putty with one part whiting, one part dry white lead.

Thursday, 11.

THE gears being ironed, the body may now be given to the smith for hanging up. Remember it is always best to have the body ironed before the roughstuff is rubbed, for, if the smith happens to burn or otherwise injure the paint, it can be easily repaired; and there are few who can iron off a job without a "shop mark" on some part.

Friday, 12.

TO-DAY the job is in the smith's hands, and we have time to note down a few *timely* remarks. It is seldom that we see a carriage gear "cleaned up" as it should be for the painter. The smith, so long as he gets the irons on and screwed up, seems to care for nothing more. We see clips drawn down into the beds, nuts turned down into the rims, making a hole for the painter to putty up, and many other "actual deeds of carelessness," left for the painter to "smooth over." Can't we do better on this job?

Saturday, 13.

THE job having now returned to the paint-shop, unhung, well filed and sandpapered, our first operation will be to repair any burned or broken parts of the surface, by putty and roughstuff. The gears should now have a thin coat of P. W. F. brushed on and well wiped off with rags. Remember, that a good wiping off will hasten operations, for the P. W. F. will be ready for the next coat much sooner. Go over wood and iron alike, and stand the job in a warm place to dry. A coat of "stain" may be added to the body late in the afternoon.

Monday, 15.

THE gears may now be puttied or "glazed over," with soft putty. But bear in mind that the less putty you use, and yet "level up" imperfections, the better. The body is ready for rubbing out of roughstuff. For this purpose we advise the use of prepared rubbing-stone (grade 3, II.) for first rubbing; then, to finish and make a smooth surface, choose some good lump pumice-stone. Keep a plenty of water on the work, for if the stone is allowed to get dry it will be apt to scratch the surface. There being but two coats of roughstuff on the job, great care must be taken not to "rub through."

Tuesday, 16.

PUTTY up any imperfections on gears, and smooth down same with the back of a piece of sandpaper, or a leather. The putty being quick drying, and there being but little used, we need not apply a second coat of P.W. F., as in the case of first-class work, and, therefore, a coat of color is next in order—(say black). This we will lay on as smoothly as possible, with a camel's hair brush.

Wednesday, 17.

THE body being rubbed and well *dried out*, is now ready for color.

DECEMBER, 1879.

A coat of lampblack will serve well for a foundation or ground coat for any dark color, and this we now apply. The gears are ready for the first coat of color-and-varnish, which may be laid on "full," with a varnish brush. The color and varnish should be quite *strong* with color. Use Valentine's Quick Leveling Varnish.

Thursday, 18.

THIS morning a coat of ivory black color may be put upon the body, after it has been well rubbed over with some half-worn sandpaper. After noon dust off lightly, and lay on a medium heavy coat of Valentine's Black-Japan, using varnish tools, and "dressing" it as little as possible. (See Saturday Feb. 23d.)

Friday, 19.

THE gears should now be lightly rubbed with pumice-stone and water and prepared for striping or ornamenting. Eastern builders make all their work quite plain, and would, no doubt, in this case stripe the gears with a single fine line of red, or blue, or some simple color, while fashion in the West demands light colors and much ornamentation. The face of the spokes, the ends of the spring-bars and bolt-heads, would, probably be gilded, or broad stripes take the place of the Eastern fine lines.

Saturday, 20.

TO-DAY flat down the black Japan on body, with pumice-stone and water. *Do not rub too much.* If, as you should have done, you have got a *clean* coat on, a very light rub will remove the gloss, and prepare the surface for the second coat of black Japan. When nicely flatted and washed clean, put on the black Japan, having a little, (say 10 per cent.) hard-drying body varnish added, to increase its flowing qualities and to give it a superior hardness for rubbing down for the finishing coat.

Monday, 22.

GIVE this day for the drying of the black Japan on the body, and the striping on the gears. The trimmer may take measurements for cushion, fall, carpet, etc., and we will find it a good plan to have the shafts trimmed before the finishing coat is put on.

Tuesday, 23.

THIS will be a good day for putting on the final coat of varnish, using medium drying body and elastic gear varnishes. Look to it that the heat and ventilation of your room is all that can be desired, and you need have no fears of any "deviltry" occuring with the varnish.

Wednesday, 24.

HANG up the job, black off bolt-heads, and run the carriage into the show room or other *warm* place to harden.

Thursday, 25.

DR. FRANKLIN wishes all his friends a Merry Christmas.

Friday, 26.

THE world wants more sunshine in its disposition, in its business, in its charities. For ten thousand of the aches and pains and irritations of men and women, we recommend sunshine. It soothes better than morphine, it stimulates better than champagne. Florence Nightingale used it on Crimean battle fields. Take it anywhere and everywhere, it is good for all the ills that flesh is heir to; and *who*, above all others, needs it more than the painter who strives to do good work. He smiles with pleasure to see a sunny day, and he feels that heaven itself is only more sunshine.

Saturday, 27.

POLISHING VARNISH.—In polishing the inside fittings and glass frames of heavy jobs it is necessary that the varnish be well hardened; and Valentine's Quick Leveling Varnish has proved excellent for this work. From three to five coats of this varnish well rubbed, after each coat is dry, and then polished with oil and rotten-stone, will make a first-class piece of work—try it!

DECEMBER, 1879.

Monday, 29.

"WHICH is the healthier, Oolong or Hyson?" asks a correspondent. That's a question we don't care to teacup at the present time.

JOHN PARTRIDGE, of Pittsburgh, was thrush-ed into jail for thirty days for creating a disturbance. The sentence didn't make him quail, however.

Tuesday, 30.

B. C. AND V.—The cause of black color-and-varnish going "silky" is due to the oil in the black. Quick black may be added to varnish for this purpose, but oily black never; and the best way is to grind black directly in varnish, then dilute with more varnish to make color-and-varnish. We perfer black Japan in all cases to black C. and V. Have you ever tried it? The best way is to use Valentine's "Black Color-and-Varnish," in which you will find the Drop Black so fine that it remains in suspension a long time, and even when it has been standing long enough to settle, it will readily mix by shaking.

Wednesday, 31.

GENERAL RULES.—1st. Let the ground or surface to be painted be, at the start, perfectly clean, smooth and well dried. 2d. See that your colors are well ground and duly mixed. 3d. Do not mix much more or any less paint than is necessary for immediate use. 4th. Keep the paint well stirred while the work is going on. 5th. Have your paint of the proper thickness, and lay it on as evenly as possible. 6th. Do not apply a coat of paint until the preceding one is properly dry. 7th. Do not, if possible, employ a light color over a darker one. 8th. Do not add dryers to colors long before they are used. 9th Avoid using an excess of dryers. "Enough is as good as a feast" should be your motto in this connection. 10th. Always keep dry pigments in a *dry place*, as dampness will affect the shade of colors, and also their drying qualities.

NONE are too wise to be mistaken.—*Barrow.*

PREDJUDICE is the child of ignorance.—*Haslett.*

THE right kind of a boy with a pea-shooter can take a man's mind off his business troubles and politics quicker than anything else in this bleak, cold world.

THE Old Year can never more come back again. To us it is buried, buried forever. The joys it has given us, the sorrows it has filled our hearts with, we can now only remember as though it were but a dream of yesterday. The sunshine that glowed in our pathway, the blue sky that smiled over our heads, the brooklet that babbled its song in our ears, and the winds that sighed in the wildwood to us, may seem to-day just the same as they used to, but yet the shadow of the Old Year has ceased to fall over them forevermore.

1880   JAN.   1880

"THAT painter's work will stand the test
Who strives to do his work the best."

Sun.	Mon.	Tue.	Wed.	Thu.	Fri.	Sat.
--	--	--	--	1	2	3
4	5	6	7	8	9	10
11	12	13	14	15	16	17
18	19	20	21	22	23	24
25	26	27	28	29	30	31
--	--	--	--	--	--	--

Thursday, 1.

BE FRANK.

Whatever you are, be frank, boys :
'Tis better than money and rank, boys ;
  Still cleave to the right ;
  Be lovers of light ;
Be open, above-board, and frank, boys.

Friday, 2.

THIS is the time for general retrospection. Let us look back and see what we have accomplished in the way of improvement since the 7th day of July last, when we begun a new era in our paint-shop.

Has the "American Method of Painting" proved a success?

Have we followed the track marked out for us in aiming for that goal, without stepping once aside and into the old routine?

Has our work been less laborious upon the workmen, and are they pleased to continue with the process of painting?

Have my profits been larger than in years gone by?

These and many other questions we may ask ourselves, and then placing the answers aye and nay side by side upon paper, we may easily determine what is best for the coming six months.

Saturday, 3.

The deviltries of cold weather upon varnish and paint are now at their meridian. Our paint-rooms are warm, well ventilated and clean. Our varnish-room is as good in its general arrangements as one could wish for, and we can almost bid defiance to the evil one in so far as his agency goes regarding the quality of our work. But we have another source of trouble. We find that ill-ventilated and poorly-contrived stables, ignorant coachmen, or careless boys, are, at this time of the year, as great pests as flies in summer. The first, ruining our work by covering it with ammonia fumes or dust, with dampness and lime salts from its walls of stone or brick. The second, flooding our glossy coating with water at or near the boiling point, or else allowing frozen water and mud to remain as an outside covering to the wheels and under gears, for days together. How can we prevent this?

Monday, 5.

Give a warm, friendly grip of the hand to any poor boy below you, struggling to climb up. I do not know a meaner thing than for a boy to try to keep such a companion down by ridicule or petty annoyances. It argues a narrow, coarse-grained nature and an unfeeling spirit, none of which are counted legal tender for the world's favor. A manly boy is above such meanness. It is yourself and not your friends or your opportunities that will make or unmake your fortune in this world. If you feel that there is a margin for improvement in your case, waste no time in delays. The way is a very plain one, and most pleasant and profitable to walk in.—*Hub.*

Tuesday, 6.

"The Hub" Chart on the Preservation of Carriages should be freely circulated in every neighborhood,—posted in every stable and carriage-house,—framed and placed conspicuously upon the walls of every office, until the people are educated up to that standard of keeping a carriage which we, the carriage-painters, possess. If you have not seen a copy, address a postal to "The Hub," 323 Pearl-street, N. Y., and get one by return mail.

Wednesday, 7.

HOW TO RUB OUT VARNISH RUNS.—Take a lump of pumice-stone and face it down with a file, then rub the face with another piece of pumice-stone, after which rub the face with a piece of castile soap, then apply a little ground pumice-stone, when the run can be cut down without clogging the stone, also the brush marks can be readily faced down.

Thursday, 8.

AN Irishwoman, at a loss for a word, went into a drug store, and looking much puzzled, said she had come for some medicine, but the name had slipped her memory "intirely," but sounded like "pappy in the garret." The druggist, willing to make a sale, hit upon paregoric. "Indeed, then, that's it," said she, obtaining the medicine, and going away delighted that she had come so near the *right word*.

Friday, 9.

GOLD BRONZE.—The best way to use bronze is to put it on dry over gilding-size, using a piece of chamois or plush as a rubber; this gives a metallic luster not obtained when the bronze is mixed as paint. My experience with bronze mixed in this way has been limited to small ornaments only, and I can not, therefore, speak with certainty as regards striping; but an esteemed "brother brush" of Philadelphia, familiarly known to the trade as Uncle Joe Edwards, says of it: "Mix the bronze with Japan Gold-size in a glass or china cup, and set it aside, and in a few hours the mixture will be found covered with a greenish film that looks something like verdigris; pour this off, and then stripe with it, and the bronze will not darken for a long time, and, in many cases will not turn at all." I would add that bronze is liable to turn dark, when it is put on to size that is not dry enough to receive it, in which case it is technically "drowned" or swallowed up by the "wet" size. It will also darken when varnished over with English varnish, but no grade of American varnish seems inclined to affect it. In the foreign varnish, there seems to be some agent present which acts like an acid upon the metal dust, corroding it and forming verdigris, but by giving the work a coat of American varnish first, and then English finishing, if *the latter must* be used, no trouble will be experienced.

Saturday, 10.

THE young ladies at a certain seminary are not allowed to ride with a gentleman, unless he is a near relative or an accepted suitor. Here is a case where the governing authority was circumvented. One of the young ladies asked for permission to ride with a gentleman. "You know the regulations of the institution," was the answer, "Is he your father?" "No." "Is he your brother?" "No." "Are you engaged to him?" "No, but I expect to be before I get back." This answer carried the day.

Monday, 12.

SANDPAPERING THE WORK WHEN APPLYING P. W. F.—The object in rubbing the P. W. F. with sandpaper is to remove the fuzz, which always rises on moistened wood, which fuzz, being very fine and soft, is partially rubbed into the pores, thereby assisting as a filler; and besides, the rubbing forces the liquid still further into the wood. To simply lay a thin coating of P. W. F. on the wood, and allow it to "soak in," is not the proper way to prime a carriage body; and if you do not do the work properly, how can you expect good results?

Tuesday, 13.

APPLYING PERMANENT WOOD FILLING.—*In no case should P. W. F. be reduced with turpentine or oil,* but it should be applied in its pure state. The parts of the body which are covered with canvas or muslin should be primed with "slush," and not with P. W. F., as too great an amount of the latter would be absorbed and kept in contact with the glue, which would be liable to soften the latter; but in no case will P. W. F. affect other glued parts of the job. To apply the P. W. F., take an ordinary clean bristle paint-brush, and, dipping it into the liquid, spread it on a portion of the body (say on a side panel), giving a moderately heavy coat. No great care need be taken to spread this evenly; it may even be daubed on roughly, for immediately afterward we proceed to rub the part thus coated with a piece of fine sandpaper, or, still better, some that is half-worn, with just sufficient grit to remove the fuzz of the wood. Then wipe off all the superfluous P. W. F. varnish, and our only means of doing this is by the use of a porous material called roughstuff. Now, if we should mix this roughstuff with sufficient oil or varnish to make it anti-porous, we would be unable to rub it to a smooth surface; so, to carry out our plan, we have to coat the rubbed roughstuff surface with P. W. F., and we do this in the same manner as if priming, excepting that no sandpaper is used. This will effectually close the pores of the roughstuff, and at the same time securely bind or cement the paint into a homogeneous mass, giving us a marble-like surface on which to spread the color.

Wednesday, 14.

A LADY from the country who has lately become a resident of the city was very much troubled at her son's long absence from home the other evening. A neighbor calling, suggested that he had gone to see the elephant. "Ah," said the other, with a sigh of relief, "why didn't he tell me? I haven't any objection to his seeing the elephant, and didn't even know it was in town."

Thursday, 15.

IVORY BLACK.—There are those who purchase prepared black with the expectation of getting an article ready for spreading with the brush, and when they find that the paint is *too thick* and requires thinning to a proper consistency for the work in hand, they are at a loss what to do with it—whether to add oil, turpentine, varnish or Japan; and in some cases the paint is spoiled by the vehicle used to dilute it. To such people we would say: Open the paint can and take out into a clean cup the amount likely to be used, close the can again and set it away; next, add to the paint in your cup just enough turpentine to soften it or thin it to a cream-like consistency, stirring it well meanwhile with a flattened stick or a putty-knife. Now, take up a drop or two and apply it to the thumb-nail of the left hand, brushing it down level and thin with the finger—blow the breath upon it to hasten evaporation of its parts, and in a second it will appear quite dry, and "dead" or "flat;" this is called "quick color" and is suitable for any hurried job ; but to make it perfect for coloring over the panels of a carriage or on gears, add to the paint now thinned a very small quantity of raw linseed oil—say a tablespoonful to a pint of paint, stir all well together, and then try the thumb-nail test ; the paint should now appear to dry with a subdued gloss—not so "dead" as before, and if found so it is in proper condition for laying on. Be careful in the use of oil in color: too much is worse than none at all, while the proper quantity adds durability to the work, and gives ease in spreading it evenly.

Friday, 16.

"Good morning, Donnelly, I hear your daughter has a baby ; is it a boy or a girl ?" "Sure, miss, and it's meself that doesn't yet know for the life of me if I'm a grandfather or grandmother, bedad."

The major (rocking Nellie on his knee for Aunt Mary's sake): "I suppose this is what you like, Nellie ?" "Yes, it's very nice, but I rode on a real donkey yesterday—I mean one with four legs, you know."

Saturday, 17.

KEEPING CUPS.—The best method of keeping cups is to have a strong sheet-iron pan or box filled with potash water, into which the empty cups are placed, and when wanted for use, a good washing with clean water will at any time give you a perfectly clean cup. It is well to have plenty of cups on hand, for a scarcity often causes waste of paint. Varnish-cups should have a *flat side* made on the top edge, that one may wipe the brushes over, without fear of rounding them (see illustration), and at least three cups should be used in

varnishing a body, in order to keep the varnish for the particularly difficult or prominent parts, perfectly clean, and free from air bubbles.

Monday, 19.

A placard in the window of a patent medicine vender, in Paris, reads as follows: "The public are requested not to mistake this shop for that of *another* quack, just opposite."

JANUARY, 1880.

Tuesday, 20.

PUTTY FOR GLASS FRAMES.—It is found troublesome to keep ordinary putty on glass frames, and in hearses, from chipping out, and we therefore add here a receipt for making a putty that will remain where it is put. Take a piece of plush or velvet and draw out the warp, leaving a fine flocking (short threads), mix this flocking with your ordinary putty, and use in the usual manner. The short threads serve the same purpose as hair mixed in plaster by the mason, binding the particles together and effectually preventing chipping or breaking out in small pieces. The large glasses in hearses should be allowed to rest on a rubber strip, and then puttied in place with putty made as above ; together with small strip of wood screwed solidly to the frame.

Wednesday, 21.

WHY is a solar eclipse like a woman whipping her boy ? Because it's a hiding of the sun.

WHEN will there be only twenty-five letters in the alphabet ? When you and I are made one.

WHAT is the difference between the North and South pole ? All the difference in the world.

Thursday, 22.

FORMULA FOR MIXING PAINT.—Soften the dry powder into a mush-like condition, by the addition of Crown Coach Japan, stirring it well with a stick until thoroughly mixed. Then reduce to a milk-like consistency with turpentine. This gives us what is known as " Quick Color " and is useful in hurried work ; but for good *color*, add to the mixture a few drops (say a tablespoonful to a pint) of raw linseed oil, and test the drying by the thumb-nail test spoken of on page 59.

Friday, 23.

SELF-RESPECT.—Always remember no one can really debase you but yourself. Slander, satire, falsehood, injustice—these can never rob you of your manhood. Men may lie about you, they may denounce you, they may cherish suspicions manifold, they may make your failings the target of their wit or cruelty ; never be alarmed ; never swerve an inch from the line your judgment and conscience have marked out for you. They cannot, by all their efforts, take away your knowledge of yourself, the purity of your motives, the integrity of your character, and the generosity of your nature. While these are left, you are, in point of fact, unharmed.

Saturday, 24.

CLEANLINESS.—The paint-rooms should be swept often, to remove loose dirt and lint, for the tires of wheels have just enough paint on the edge to attract light dirt, many times causing a bad piece of work, which would have been avoided had the floor been clean. In winter, scatter snow over the floor and sweep the room before the snow melts to water. In summer, sprinkle well and let remain until a portion of the water has evaporated and the floor is simply damp. You can then sweep without rising dust.

Monday, 26.

"HABIT" is hard to overcome. If you take off the first letter it does not change it "a bit." If you take off another, you still have a "bit" left. If you take off still another, the whole of "it" remains. If you take off another, it is not "t" totally used up. All of which goes to show that if you wish to be rid of a "habit" you must throw it off altogether.

Tuesday, 27.

THE painter should avoid using a greater number of pigments in mixing colors than are absolutely necessary to produce the color required. Another fact is, that *old* pigments are preferable to new ones, on account of their better drying and being less likely to be adulterated.

Wednesday, 28.

THERE hasn't been a saloon in Starkville, Miss., for the last twenty-five years. But listen—sh–h–h—you can get it at the druggist's.

"I AM busy ploughing and cannot entertain company," was the substance of a note sent by a Michigan belle in reply to an intimation that a gentlemen desired to see her.

JANUARY, 1880.

Thursday, 29.

VARNISHING.—When varnishing bodies that have small panels, it will be found best to flow on a medium heavy coat to several panels before attempting to lay it off or "dress it," else a greater amount of time will be necessary to complete the work, and then, it will not be done so well. Finishing varnish may be flowed all over a wheel before laying it off, providing the varnish is of the proper kind, and the room is of the right temperature.

Friday, 30.

A WISE "TOUCHSTONE."—A poor beggar in Paris, being hungry, stayed so long in a cook's shop who was doing up meat, that his stomach was satisfied with only the smell thereof. The choleric, covetous cook demanded of him to pay for his breakfast. The poor man denied it, and it was referred to the decision of the next man that should pass by, who chanced to be a most notorious idiot. He determined that the poor man's money should be put betwixt two empty dishes, and the cook recompensed by its jingling, as he was satisfied with only the smell of the cook's meat.

Saturday, 31.

GILDING-SIZE.—Take permanent wood filling (light shade) one part, Crown Coach Japan two parts, and mix them well together in a bottle. This can then be set away for use at any time, as the mixture improves by age. If this size dries too quickly, or too slowly, add the P. W. F. to lengthen, or the Japan to shorten the time of setting and drying ready for gilding over. Do not lay gold leaf or bronze upon size until the latter is *almost* dry, *i. e.*, has a very "tacky" feeling.

"THIS is George the Fourth," said an exhibitor of waxwork for the million, at a penny each, pointing to a very slim figure with a theatrical crown on his head. "I thought he was a very stout man," observed a spectator. "Werry likely," replied the man, shortly, not approving of the comment of his visitor, "but if you'd a been here without wittles half so long as he has, you'd been twice as thin."

THE NAKED TRUTH.—A policeman found a boy bathing in a slip, near the foot of Randolph-street, and he called to the lad to come out and be arrested like a man for breaking the ordinance.

1880   FEB.   1880

"For age and want save what you may,
No morning sun lasts a whole day."—*Franklin*.

Sun.	Mon.	Tue.	Wed.	Thu.	Fri.	Sat.
1	2	3	4	5	6	7
8	9	10	11	12	13	14
15	16	17	18	19	20	21
22	23	24	25	26	27	28
29	--	--	--	--	--	--
--	--	--	--	--	--	--

Monday, 2.

BE BRAVE.

Whatever you are, be brave, boys!
The liar's a coward and knave, boys;
  Though clever at ruses,
  And sharp at excuses,
He's a sneaking and pitiful knave, boys.

Tuesday, 3.

PRIMING.—A priming, to be durable, should unite with the wood—grasping, as it were, the fibers, and penetrating into the pores, filling them, preventing the entrance of moisture, and thereby aiding to sustain the subsequent coats. At the same time it should be composed of materials which, when dry or oxidised into resins, will possess sufficient elasticity to allow a slight change in the wood, such as that given by severe jars, or by the expansion or contraction caused by a variation in temperature, without cracking.

Wednesday, 4.

CAPT. SI. JONES says, "Harmony of colors is the *something* about a carriage which even the uncultivated buyer appreciates, though he may not know what hit him."

"It is no disgrace to make a mistake once in a while, but it is a disgrace to let such mistakes, when known, go out into the world."

Thursday, 5.

PAINTING ZINC.—It is frequently the case where the zinc panels or sides of a business wagon are painted in the ordinary way, i. e., with oil-lead, etc., the paint chips off or flakes from the zinc, and the painter is called to account for it. To overcome the difficulty, first coat the zinc with Light Permanent Wood Filling, and wipe off with clean rags, leaving a thin film of the material only, upon the surface, give from twenty-four to forty-eight hours for drying, then proceed in the usual manner to paint the work.

Friday, 6.

MIXING VARNISHES.—It is, as a general thing, a dangerous proceeding to mix one grade of varnish with another, as the liability to cause deviltries is very great. But with Valentine's varnishes the case is different, and they may be mixed by the painter, with judgment, for it must be remembered that the addition of a lower grade of varnish will reduce the durability in like proportion. The painter who fully understands the working of these varnishes will be able to grade them to suit any requirement, a feature which in some shops is of the greatest importance.

Saturday, 7.

FROM Oshkosh: A man in the town of Rushford killed another man's dog. The son of the man whose dog was killed therefore proceeded to whip the man who killed the dog of the man he was son of.

The man who was the son of the man whose dog was killed was arrested by the man who was assaulted by the son of the man whose dog the man assaulted and killed.

Monday, 9.

CHINESE VERMILION.—Some years ago Chinese vermilion was considered the best red for striping, and the enormous demand for it caused extra production, while but a small portion of the pigment came from China. A miserable imitation was put upon the market, and, possibly, it is some of this "counterfeit" vermilion that you have been using. It is not used to any great extent by our city painters, the *English light vermilion* being much better and sold at a less price. This red will mix and flow freely in japan or oil.

Tuesday, 10.

SHARP-eyed men of business take note of a boy's general bearing, in making up their estimate of what he is worth. "I would give more for what my eyes can tell me about a boy in ten minutes, than all the letters of recommendation he can bring me," said a man who had just selected a lad from a crowd that had applied for the place. A straightforward manly bearing will help any lad to win his way in the world, while a slip-shod, sneaking manner usually suggests to the observer a corresponding character.

Wednesday, 11.

PUTTYING.—It has been found best in practice to sink the heads of nails, brads, or screws quite deep into the wood, then to wet the places with hot water slightly, so that the wood will swell over them and partly fill the hole. Then putty the holes, during the course of painting, with more than sufficient to make the place level with the surface. All large holes should be but partly filled at first in order to dry hard way through, and at the second puttying should be filled more than full, as above.

Thursday, 12.

TRUE manliness is not a garment you can put off and on like your

Sunday coat. It must have its foundation in the inner man, or it will be a flimsy sham that will deceive nobody. Cultivate noble, manly sentiments, for, "as a man thinketh in his heart, so is he." If these have a dwelling place in your breast, they will shine out in your daily life, and be known and read of all men.

Friday, 13.

RUBBING THROUGH.—There is a certain amount of assimilation between coats of varnish, sufficient to cause them to closely adhere one to the other, providing the proper harmony exists in the varnishes, but this is not perceptible to the rubber, and he may easily rub through one, two or three coats and be able to see each separate layer. Care should *always* be taken not to rub through a coat of varnish, but no *very* great damage will be done if by accident or want of care the under coats are laid bare, except it be in the last rubbing—just before the finishing coat is applied—when the spot or spots are liable to show in certain positions of the carriage.

Saturday, 14.

A MAN, to save money, may starve himself to death, and the consequence is that he is too weak to do work. He has not economized, for the result shows a waste of health and strength. A shop cannot be kept open without goods : a paper could not succeed without articles to make it attractive, and products could not grow in an unfruitful soil. How then can a man expect to keep himself in bodily health without proper nourishment? When studying for the best mode to economize we should ascertain to a certainty that our decision is true wisdom, not niggardly folly.*

Monday, 16.

WHITE-LEAD.—We have never recommended the use of English white-lead, and see no reason why it should be better than any pure white-lead made in this country. "Atlantic," "Jewett's," and "Pittsburgh B. B." are all good brands, and we would never look further for lead to use on carriage work. The "American Method of Carriage-painting" occasions the use of white-lead only in the rough-stuff (excepting for colors), and the brands mentioned above are used by most painters. The application of from three to five coats of lead-color to a body or gear is, to-day, an old-fogy proceeding.

Tuesday, 17.

SOME one observes, there is a difference between a woman's smile and a man's smile. There is—a wide difference sometimes. A woman's "smile" is seldom stronger than soda-water, while the man's "smile" is seldom weaker than whisky and water.

Wednesday, 18.

PREPARED ROUGHSTUFF.—No matter how good a receipt the painter may have, or how carefully he may mix his roughstuff, it is impossible for him to measure the proportions in a small way as can be done in a large one. To a barrel of pigment we can easily add 10 gallons of each of the liquids used, and duplicate the mixture at different times, but the painter cannot so easily proportion the ingredients in the cup ; therefore at one time his paint will be more or less elastic than at another, and it is well known what effect a coat of extra elastic paint will have if placed under or between harder and less elastic ones. Besides, it is much handier to have roughstuff ready at all times, saying nothing of the cleanliness thereby gained, and the economy in time.

Thursday, 19.

(HERR PUMPERNICKLE, having just played a composition of his own, bursts into tears.) Chorus of friends : Oh, what is the matter ? What can we do for you ? Herr Pumpernickle : Ach ! nossen ! nossen ! Bot ven I hear really coot music, zen must I always veep.—*Punch.*

Friday, 20.

DRYING OUT.—The "drying out" of the body, after it has been rubbed out of roughstuff is of vital importance, and should not be neglected. Roughstuff, providing it is *good rubbing* roughstuff, is necessarily *porous*, no matter what pigment or vehicle is used, and the water used in rubbing is consequently absorbed by it ; therefore, it is essential, after the moisture has thus entered the paint, that time and a good position be given the work for "drying out" before another application of paint is made.

Saturday, 21.

"WHAT gender is sugar?" asked a teacher of the grammar class. "What kind of sugar?" asked a boy. "What kind?" repeated the teacher, "What has that to do with it?" "Why, if it's maple sugar it's feminine gender," said the boy. "Why feminine gender?" asked the teacher, with a puzzled face. "Because you can't tell its age," promptly replied the boy.

Monday, 23.

ALL honor to him who was "first in war, first in peace, and first in the hearts of his countrymen."

"If my endeavors to avert the evil with which the country was threatened, by a deliberate plan of tyranny, should be crowned with the success that is wished, the praise is due to the GRAND ARCHITECT of the universe, who did not see fit to suffer his superstructure of justice to be subjected to the ambition of the Princes of this world, or to the rod of oppression in the hands of any power upon earth."—*Geo. Washington.*

Tuesday, 24.

Two men were riding in the cars on the Danbury Railway, the other morning, when one asked the other if he had a pleasant place of residence. "Yes," was the reply, "we have seven nice large rooms over a store." "Over a store! I shouldn't think that would be a quiet place." "Oh, it is quiet enough. The folks don't advertise." "Ah, I see," said his friend, in a tone of relief.—*Danbury News.*

Wednesday, 25.

GROUND COLORS.—The ground upon which a color is laid will in many cases affect the tone of that color: especially is this the case with light colors, such as drab, French gray, etc., although these seem to be solid or opaque colors. Few would believe that when two good coats of ultramarine blue are laid over a bright chrome yellow ground, that the blue will appear purer or richer than if laid over a lead, or light blue, but it is so.

FEBRUARY, 1880.

Thursday, 26.

ONE of the Norwich steamers had struck, and, while the passengers were hurriedly making preparations for their safety, a fat old Dutchman seized a life-preserver, and, trying it on, began to fill it, blowing till he was red in the face with his efforts. "Hallo," said a bystander, "you can't fill that thing; there's a big hole in it." A blank look came over the Dutchman's face. "Mein Gott, is dat so; den I better keeps my wind in me."

Friday, 27.

CANS FOR THE BENCH.—We often see upon the paint-bench those long slim varnish cans used for holding turpentine, Japan, and oil, and knowing the trouble experienced by the paint mixer, oftentimes, when he attempts to pour "just a little" of their contents into his paint, we take this opportunity to advise against their use. An apprentice-boy not long since ruined a pint cup full of carmine color, by trying to pour a *very little* oil upon the top of it to prevent its drying up. The can being unwieldy, tipped a *little too far* and—well the carmine was thrown out over the floor and its place supplied by a mass of raw linseed oil, which of course was the ruination of the whole lot of color. Discard them at once! and purchase two or three old-fashioned oil cans having a long spout to pour from, or else suffer waste and provocation at frequent intervals.

Saturday, 28.

"EPHRAIM." said Simon, "what does a young fellow look like when gallanting his sweetheart through a shower?" "Why," replied Ephraim, "he has very much the appearance of a rain beau."

"CHARLIE, what is it that makes you so sweet?" said a loving mother to her little boy as she pressed him to her bosom. "I dess when Dod made me out of dust, he put a little sugar in," said Charlie

A MAN who cheats in short measure is a measureless rogue. If in whiskey, then he is a rogue in spirit. If by falsifying his accounts, then he is an unaccountable rogue. If he gives a bad title to land, then he is a rogue indeed. If he gives short measure in wheat, then he is a rogue in grain.

SYNOPSIS
OF THE
AMERICAN METHOD ON BODIES.

1st day,	Apply P. W. F., and wipe off, -	For drying, give	48 hours.
3d "	First coat of roughstuff, a little oily, -	- "	48 "
5th "	2d " " ordinary, -	- "	24 "
6th "	3d " " "	- "	24 "
7th "	4th " " "	- "	24 "
8th "	Stain coat over roughstuff, -	- - "	24 "
9th "	Rub down with pumice-stone.		
10th "	P. W. F. rubbed over and well wiped off,	- "	48 "
12th "	1st coat of color or lampblack, -	- - "	24 "
13th "	2d " " ivory black, -	- - "	24 "
14th "	1st coat of color-and-varnish or Black Japan,	"	48 "
16th "	2d " " " "	"	48 "
18th "	3d " " " "	"	48 "
20th "	Finishing coat of Wearing Body Varnish.		

ON GEARS.

1st day,	P.W.F. put on the completed gear and wipe off,	give	48 hours.
3d "	Putty up all open-grained places, -	- "	24 "
4th "	Sandpaper, putty, and put on P. W. F. again,	"	48 "
6th "	Apply color or lampblack, -	- - - "	24 "
7th "	Apply color-and-varnish, quite strong, -	- "	48 "
9th "	Rub and give second coat of color-and-varnish,	"	48 "
11th "	Rub down, stripe, and ornament, -	- "	24 "
12th "	Give coat of rubbing varnish, -	- - "	48 "
14th "	Finish with Elastic Gear Varnish.		

The above time is given as the minimum or shortest possible time to do a first-class job, but as the painter will generally have more time to spare upon the job, he may divide it, giving the extra time for the P. W. F. and the varnish coats to harden.

1880 MARCH. 1880

*" If you would have your work well done,
Be sure your work is well begun."*

Sun.	Mon.	Tue.	Wed.	Thu.	Fri.	Sat.
- -	1	2	3	4	5	6
7	8	9	10	11	12	13
14	15	16	17	18	19	20
21	22	23	24	25	26	27
28	29	30	31	- -	- -	- -
- -	- -	- -	- -	- -	- -	- -

Monday, 1.

BETTER LATE THAN NEVER.

Life is a race, where some succeed,
  While others are beginning ;
'Tis luck at times, at others speed,
  That gives an early winning.
But if you chance to fall behind,
  Ne'er slacken your endeavor,
But keep this wholesome truth in mind—
  'Tis better late than never.

Tuesday, 2.

FRANKLIN AND THE LIGHTNING.—The celebrated experiment of Ben Franklin, by which he demonstrated the identity of lightning and the common electric spark, was performed by him in June, 1752, at Philadelphia, Pa. Having made a cross-stick kite, he covered it with a silk handkerchief, instead of paper, so that it would stand rain, attached a tail, etc. The upper end of the cross had an iron point, connected by a string to the usual kite-cord, which was of hemp. To the lower end of the cord an iron key was attached, and to that a short length of silk ribbon as a non-conductor, by which the kite-string could be safely held in the hand. On the approach of a thunder storm he proceeded to a common near the city, and, with the assistance of his son, sent up the kite. Ere long the thunder cloud approached, the electricity came down the kite-string, and Franklin, standing under a shed, received the electric sparks through his knuckles, which he applied to the key, and charged his Leyden jar by putting his conductors in contact with the key. The rain then fell, which improved the conductivity of the kite-cord, and the electricity appeared in increased quantity. The news of the wonderful experiment rapidly spread over the world, and was extensively repeated. In France, Professor Romas made a kite seven feet high, with a fine wire interwoven in the string. The kite was raised five hundred and fifty feet, and is alleged to have yielded flashes of electric fire ten feet in length. In St. Petersburg, Professor Richman, while attempting to repeat Franklin's experiments, received so heavy a charge of electricity that he fell dead. This was in 1793.

Wednesday, 3.

WHEN others shunned the murky sky
　Where flash on flash was bright'ning,
Great Franklin went to fly his kite,
　And bottled up the lightning.

And since his time, when cares oppress,
　And hard the times are tight'ning,
The painter seeks to drown his woes
　In draughts of "bottled lightning."

When badly tattered—his warm heart,
　A place for grief to rankle in—
He takes the "lightning," flies his kite,
　And thinks himself a Franklin.

Thursday, 4.

THE DEVILTRIES OF VARNISH.—" The defects known as pitting, pin-holing, curdling, wrinkling, enameling, drawing up, and going stringy, are mainly due to the same general causes, namely : 1. Change in the atmosphere from dry to damp ; 2. Mixing two kinds of varnish of different grades or different makers ; 3. Excessive heat or cold ; 4.

Varnishing over color or varnish which has not become sufficiently dry ; or, 5, which is sweaty ; 6. Varnishing with the floor very wet, or damp and cold from other causes ; 7. Placing cold or damp varnish on warm panels, or *vice versa* (by 'damp varnish' I mean varnish that has been kept in a cellar or other damp or cold place) ; and 8, another common cause is the lack of proper ventilation, and of maintaining a uniform temperature."

Friday, 5.

To polish a carriage-body, proceed as follows : First, be sure to have at least three coats of some hard-drying varnish (American, not English), and give at least two weeks' time for it to become *hard*, then rub the surface with pulverized pumice-stone and water in the usual manner, until the nibs and imperfections are all removed. Next wash clean and renew the rubbing, this time using rotten-stone instead of pumice-stone, and plenty of water ; wash off with a very soft sponge, and dry carefully with the shammy. Next, take pulverized rotten-stone and sweet oil, and rub the parts until a gloss is obtained. Use soft woolen rags for the rubber. To remove the oil from the work, take wheat flour and a soft piece of silk. The palm of the hand may be used effectively in producing the desired luster. And after all the labor thus expended, the job will not look one-half as well, neither will it be so durable as one finished with a flowing coat of Wearing Body Varnish.

Saturday, 6.

IF the painter uses the goods of several different manufacturers, he cannot put the same dependence on his work, for he knows not which is adulterated with fish or cotton-seed oil, nor what degree of assimilation or " grasping " there will be between the coats ; while with a pure and uniform oil, judiciously mixed throughout, from the foundation to the finish, he may rest assured of success, and be enabled to locate any difficulty experienced, and remedy it in the future.

Monday, 8.

COULDN'T TELL.—" Is that a friend of yours ?" asked a gentleman, pointing to a party who was sailing rapidly down the street. "Can't tell you till next Saturday," was the answer, "I've just lent him five dollars."

Tuesday, 9.

CAMEL'S-HAIR BRUSHES or "blenders" as they are called, and other flat brushes, require no extra binding ; the former being best for laying on fine color, the painter should have a number of them on hand, that it may never be necessary to change them from one color to another, for the cleansing of a brush occasions more wear than the spreading of paint, besides a waste of turpentine.

Wednesday, 10.

When a man has a "brush on the road" it does not necessarily follow that he is driving a brougham.

N. B.—You must pronounce this last word " broom," English fashion, to get the full force of the joke.

Thursday, 11.

BRUSHES.—The cause of the hairs falling out or being worked out of brushes, particularly fitch-brushes, is attributable simply to improper or careless manufacture. Whether it is for the sake of economy or not I do not know, but many of the fitch-brushes have scarcely cement enough in them to fasten one half the hairs. Again, I have in some cases met with brushes which were made with a cement that was *soluble in varnish*, which, I have no doubt, is frequently the cause of " specky " varnish.

If the brushes are made properly, with shellac for cementing the hair, and then securely nailed, there will never be trouble with them. To remedy the evil in a brush already in use, in respect to shedding the hair, place the brush in a vise just up to the nails, and give it a pretty good squeeze ; then open the back or handle end, and fill the interior with melted shellac or resin [the former being preferable], and allow it to remain until dry.

Friday, 12.

WHEN a young man has thoroughly comprehended the fact that he knows nothing, and that, intrinsically, he is of but little value, the next lesson is that the world cares nothing for him. He is the subject of no man's overwhelming admiration ; neither petted by the one sex, nor envied by the other, he has to take care of himself. He will not be noticed till he becomes noticeable ; he will not become noticeable until he does something to prove that he is of some use to society. No recommendation or introduction will give him this ; he must do something to be recognized as somebody. There is plenty of room for *men* in the world, but there is no room for idlers. Society is not very particular what a man does, so long as he does something useful, to prove himself to be a man : but it will not take the matter on trust.

Saturday, 13.

GRINDING PIGMENTS.—Some paints are injured by grinding in the mill, or by contact with metal surfaces. Arsenic-yellow is best ground on the stone. Vermilion should not be ground, although some prefer to grind it, and then to correct the orange tint thus developed by the addition of carmine, but we can not commend that plan ; vermilion will assimilate with the vehicles and be fine enough for any purpose, providing a little time is given after mixing it, and before use.

Monday, 15.

He had made a hearty meal at a restaurant, and, rising up, he said to the cashier : "I declare, if I haven't forgotten my wallet." The cashier fired up, and hurled big words at him for full three minutes before pausing for breath. When a chance came, the stranger continued : "But I have fifty dollars here in my vest pocket." The cashier couldn't smile to save him.

Tuesday, 16.

EXTREME HEAT AND COLD.—These affect varnishes of every kind, extreme heat being more difficult to manage than extreme cold. A chill retards drying, and often causes a sandy appearance of the varnish coat. Extreme heat causes "flattening" and "silking," and sometimes other "deviltries." Steam heat, a gas stove, or a good base-burner coal stove, will prevent the chilling of the varnish, if properly used ; and a good means of ventilation will, in summer, be a safeguard against the effects of extreme heat.

Wednesday, 17.

A YOUNG lady at the late pic-nic of the New York Guild of Carriage-Makers, whose young man was engaged at the gate taking tickets, was heard to remark: "Every cart or wagon wheel has six or seven felloes, and here I am at a carriage-makers' pic-nic and can't have one."

Thursday, 18.

CARMINE.—Carmine is a peculiar color to mix and apply to make a perfect job. One method is to mix and grind the pigment in pale rubbing varnish and then with turpentine. A good job can be made by using the carmine this way with one coat, over a ground color of darkened vermilion, if the job is given to a hand who is careful and knows how to apply it. Glazing over a prepared ground is the usual practice, and various shades of the color may be made by a slight change in the ground.

Friday, 19.

DRYERS may be mixed with paints at the moment of application to accelerate drying; but an excess of drying renders oils saponaceous, is inimical to drying, and injurious to the permanent texture of the work. Some colors, however, dry badly from not being sufficiently washed, and many are improved by burning, or by age. It is not always that ill-drying is attributable to the pigments or oils; the state of the weather and atmosphere have great influence thereon.

Saturday, 20.

SHOWERING CARRIAGES.—If you have a hose, use a good head of water, and throw it on full and strong for half an hour, only being careful not to allow the water to enter the carriage. Use a rose or sprinkler on your hose. The more water used, and the colder the water, the harder will the varnish become. Of course avoid letting the water freeze on the varnish. Soft water is preferable to hard, but either will do. If you have no hose, take a pail and sponge, and throw the water on with the sponge instead of rubbing. When well washed, dry off with a soft, clean chamois, bearing very lightly on the surface. Never let the drops of water remain on a carriage long after washing, as they are liable to leave spots. The carriage should be washed as soon as possible after the varnish has become perfectly dry, and this will prevent it from becoming dull if it remains in the repository, or from being mud-spotted if it goes out on the road.

Monday, 22.

Speaking of patchwork, a woman on Court street has a quilt in 573,291 pieces. She spread it out in the yard to air, and a puppy-dog played it was a bear. The puppy has been unwell since, and the woman spends a good deal of time in the yard waiting for him to come out from under the house. There will be some more of this item when he comes out.—*Rome Sentinel.*

Tuesday, 23.

"Why is Strakosch like the great Raphael?" asked a Chicago musical gentleman of an artist the other day. "I can't see any likeness," replied the artist. "Well, I'll tell you," said the musician. "You know Strakosch is a great hand to bring out prima donnas?" "Yes." "Certainly, of course," continued the musical chap; "and wasn't Raphael also a great hand to bring out prime madonnas?" The artist has not since been heard from.

Wednesday, 24.

ULTRAMARINE requires a good ground-work when used pure, and this should be as near the desired shade of finish as can be well obtained with other blues. Being a very transparent pigment the ground must be solid, for any streaks or clouds in that would show through, and great care must be taken to have the surface smooth, otherwise, in rubbing the varnish coats imperfections in colors will be made.

Thursday, 25.

Yet another warning: Joseph Bates, of Vermont, falls dead while carrying in an armful of wood. Show this paragraph to your wife. Nay, cut it out and pin it to the wood-shed door.

MARCH, 1880.

Friday, 26.

PAINTS AND VARNISHES ON BROUGHAM BODY.

Material.	No. of coats.	Weight.	Measure.	Cost.
P. W. F.	1	1 lb.	1 pt.	$.50
Roughstuff,	4	12 lbs.	6 pts.	2.00
Extra roughstuff on roof,	2	2 lbs.	1 pt.	.66
Black,	2	12 oz.	¾ pt.	.30
Panel color,	2	2 oz.		.15
Black Japan,	3	3 lbs.	3 pts.	2.00
Colar-and-Varnish,	3	½ lb.	½ pt.	.50
Finishing Varnish,	1	1¼ lbs.	1¼ pts.	1.00
	18 coats,			$7.11.

Saturday, 27.

A FARMER complains that a hook and ladder company has been organized in his neighborhood. He states that the ladder is used after dark for climbing into the hen house, after which the hooking is done.

Monday, 29.

WATER-PAILS.—There should be several pails always on hand for water used in washing and rubbing; and it is also well to keep one or two expressly for the finishing work on bodies; for pails that are used in washing the hands or face soon get begrimed with grease and dirt, and become unfit for use. Besides the working pails of the shop, there should in all cases be five or six pails—iron ones are best—placed upon a shelf in some convenient part of the shop, and kept filled with water, to be used in case of fire. A pail or two of water has often saved a carriage-factory from destruction; and it should be borne in mind that the paint-shop is always a dangerous place on account of the liability of spontaneous combustion. For this reason oily rags should never be left in the shop over night, and lampblack in papers should be kept in small quantities only, and out of the reach of direct sunlight, or where it might come in contact with oil.

MARCH, 1880.

Tuesday, 30.

THE various affinities of pigments occasion each to have its more or less appropriate dryer, and it would be a matter of useful experience if the habits of every pigment in this respect were ascertained.

Wednesday, 31.

LIGHT GROUND ROUGHSTUFF.—(For producing a hard and level surface on the bodies of cars.) This is a mixture of mineral substance, combined with great care, so as to furnish a dense body with a sharp grit. It is ground in Japan Gold-Size, varnish and the purest oil, and is superior to all shop-made roughstuff (sometimes erroneously called "fillings"), chiefly on account of its uniformity and its being ready for immediate use. When used over a priming of one coat of Light Permanent Wood Filling, the first coat should be made elastic with raw oil, and the following coats reduced with turpentine, if required for working.

N. B.—Stir well before using.

PREPARING FOR FINISHING.—In preparing a body for the last coat, there are few who take the necessary care to have a *smooth*, clean surface. If we were to look at the surface with a microscope after the rubbing with pumice-stone was completed, it would be found rough and full of deep scratches, small grains of varnish, gum, and pumice-stone here and there, and we would be surprised, perhaps, to see what we thought was a clean panel. Well, to overcome this, take pulverized *rotten-stone*, and with a clean rag and water work over the surface in the same manner as when rubbing with pumice-stone; this will level down or polish the surface nicely, and cleaner varnishing will result.

A LITERARY ice-cart driver, who had been annoyed by children who have been in the habit of pilfering his ice, now displays as a warning: "N. B." He thinks they will understand that that means "Take Notice."

ON Monday evening his wife asked him where he was going, as she observed him putting on his overcoat. "I am going to sally forth," he replied; and she warmly rejoined: "Let me catch you going with any Sally Forth."

1880 APRIL. 1880

"Get what you can, and what you get, hold;
'Tis the stone that will turn all your lead into gold."—*Franklin.*

Sun.	Mon.	Tue.	Wed.	Thu.	Fri.	Sat.
				1	2	3
4	5	6	7	8	9	10
11	12	13	14	15	16	17
18	19	20	21	22	23	24
25	26	27	28	29	30	--
--	--	--	--	--	--	--

Thursday, 1.

FLY LOW.

No summer sky so clear and bright
But that some cloud obscures;
No course in life so prosperous
But that some snare allures.
The softest, balmiest breeze may end
In fierce and raging squall—
Fly low, and if bad luck betide,
You've not so far to fall.

Friday, 2.

WHEN SHALL WE VARNISH?—This question is now the prominent one, and we will discuss for a moment its bearings upon the interests of the craft. We find, by observation of the thermometer, that the temperature of the air at night is far below that of the day, and, by a glance at the storm record, that storms of rain and snow are more severe when occurring between the setting and rising of the sun than at other times. These facts alone would lead us to do our varnishing *early in the day*, thus being able to nurse the tender material until a few hours' age had given it strength to withstand the effects of the atmosphere. But it is not the low temperature or the electricity of storms alone that we would guard against, and no matter how well the arrangements are for heating the varnish-room or for excluding cold and wind, we have an enemy lurking around us at night that is not with us during the day, and that enemy to the drying of varnish is moisture in the atmosphere.

The sun during the day evaporates this moisture, and the consequence is that the air then, instead of being highly charged with moisture (which falls as a dew, or as frost in winter), contains purer *oxygen*, by which varnish hardens with a bright luster, and in which atmosphere deviltries seldom occur.

Saturday, 3.

TOM HOOD mentions one grade of varnish in his " Song of the shirt," where he tells of a " woman *wearing body* and soul out."

ONE coat of color.—That which a modern belle puts on her face before starting for the ball.

Monday, 5.

THE LAST COAT OF VARNISH.—First have your work thoroughly clean. Pour out your varnish at least fifteen or twenty minutes before commencing to varnish. The varnish should be applied heavily, leveled by repeated brushing, and carefully examined during the operation to detect any foreign particles that may appear. A picker is used, made of a quill or whalebone, sharpened to a point, for removing the particles of dirt or gum. Having brushed on your varnish let it stand a few moments, when the bubbles will evaporate and show the particles of dirt remaining, which can be removed by the picker. The finishing strokes are then given very lightly, and when possible finish the strokes up and down. Do your varnishing in a bold, confident manner; use the brushes no more than is necessary to make the coat even, and your work will be perfect. The great secret in securing a perfectly clean piece of work, is to have the room, work, cups and brushes, etc., perfectly clean; also the clothing of the varnisher himself must be scrupulously clean, for without these precautions you will not succeed.

APRIL, 1880.

Tuesday, 6.

"Those who are determined to excel must go to their work whether willing or unwilling, morning, noon and night; and they will find it to be no play, but on the contrary, very hard labor."—*Sir Joshua Reynolds.*

"I do not know a fault or weakness of his (Reynolds) that he did not convert into something that bordered on a virtue, instead of pushing it into the confines of a vice."—*Burke.*

Wednesday, 7.

WHITE LEAD (the carbonate of lead) is a dry, crumbling substance, and owes all its durability, when mixed into paint, to the vehicles employed in mixing, the principal one being linseed oil. This latter substance being of a greasy nature, even when well prepared, as a vehicle for paints, will not dry or oxidize as rapidly as desired in these days of quick work; hence an addition of dryers is made to the paint, such as Japan, liquid dryer, gold-size, etc., and the amount of oil lessened. This forms a paint which, when dry upon the work, is not much better than the crumbling powder of white lead, possessing no elasticity, and ready to absorb the life (oil) of subsequent coats of paint and varnish. This absorption goes on through coat after coat, until the loss of oil from the finishing coat of varnish causes it to appear dull, and lessens its durability.

Thursday, 8.

Take Heed.—No matter how intimate you may be with the friend with whom you have business transactions—put your agreements in writing. How many misunderstandings arise from the loose ways in which business matters are talked over, and when each party puts his own construction, the matter is dismissed by each party with the words, "All right; all right." Frequently it turns out all wrong, and becomes a question for the lawyer and the courts. More than three-fourths of the litigation of the country would be saved if people would put down their agreements in writing and sign their names to it. Each word in our language has its peculiar meaning, and memory may by the change in a sentence, convey an entirely different idea from that intended. When once reduced to writing, ideas are fixed and expensive lawsuits are avoided.

APRIL, 1880.

Friday, 9.

BLUE AND YELLOW, mixed together, form grass greens. Black and yellow produce olive-green. There is a marked difference between the above shades of green, and it is very important for the painter to train his eye to notice this difference. If, for instance, we take Prussian blue and chrome yellow, and mix up a bright shade of green, and then, with black and yellow mix as near as possible an equally bright shade, the difference between the two will be readily noticed; but where a very dark shade of either of them has been used on the panels of two carriage bodies, not every painter will be able to distinguish between the two mixtures or colors, when but one of them is presented, so that in touching up a job the painter will fail to perceive of what it was composed—and the difference should be well studied in other colors as well, to ensure good and ready results.

Saturday, 10.

THE refinement that draws back from manual employment and prefers mental dawdling is a sham, and should not have social recognition. Better be a grimy painter, doing thorough work, than a titled officer enjoying a large income as a return for nominal services. Better be a day laborer than a pensioned loafer. Better be earning a comfortable livelihood by the sweat of one's face upon a farm, or in the kitchen, than depending on the uncertainties of desk-work in an overcrowded city. Better be a simple carpenter than a hair-splitting Scribe or Pharisee.

Monday, 12.

BLACKBOARD PAINT.—The following is a good recipe for blackboard paint: One quart of shellac dissolved in alcohol, three ounces pulverized pumice-stone, two ounces pulverized rotten-stone, four ounces lamp-black; mix the last three ingredients together, moisten a portion at a time with a little of the shellac and alcohol, grind as thoroughly as possible with a knife or spatula; after which pour in the remainder of the alcohol, stirring often to prevent settling. One quart will furnish two coats for eighty square feet of blackboard not previously painted. The preparation dries immediately, and the board may be used within an hour if necessary. No oil should be used.

APRIL, 1880.

Tuesday, 13.

A TEACHER in the Port Jervis public schools was last week explaining to the children that usually all words ending with "let" meant something small, as streamlet, rivulet, hamlet, etc. Whereupon a smart boy asked if hamlet meant a small ham.

Wednesday, 14.

HOW TO POUNCE ORNAMENTS, ETC.—First draw the desired design with a lead pencil upon writing or drawing paper, then prick each line full of pin-holes as close together as possible. Then lay the pricked pattern upon a sheet of white paper, and dust over it any dry color from a "pounce bag," and upon lifting the pattern you will find the outlines of a perfect duplicate on the white paper; by carefully preserving your pricked patterns you may use them again and again.

Thursday, 15.

"FOR want of water, I am forced to drink water; if I had water, I would drink wine." This speech is a riddle, and here is the solution. It was the complaint of an Italian vineyard man, after a long drought, and an extremely hot summer that had parched up all his grapes.

Friday, 16.

ELASTICITY ON GEARS—HARD-DRYING ON BODIES.—It is conceded by all good painters that the running gear of a carriage should be painted with elastic material throughout, to have it withstand the strain and jarring to which it is subjected, while the reverse is the case with bodies. The body should be painted with harder drying materials, for a soft, yielding foundation will greatly affect the luster of the finishing coat over a large panel, while on the gears this would not be perceptible. "Ring cracks," often seen on spokes and axle-beds, show that the painting was *too hard*, and large cracks on panels show that the foundation painting of the panel was *too soft*, or elastic.

Saturday, 17.

SIR JOSHUA REYNOLDS was asked what he mixed his colors with. "With *Brains*, sir!" was the reply.

APRIL, 1880.

BENJAMIN FRANKLIN died 1790, April 17.

A STEP in the right direction.—That which takes a man homeward at night.

Monday, 19.

BRUSHES.—For color coats, as blacks, browns, greens, etc., either on bodies or gears, use the double-thick camel's-hair blender. For lakes, vermilion, or glazing colors, use the badger-hair brush, it is superior to the fitch-hair or camel's-hair brush, and leaves the coating more even, neither showing streaks nor laps. For varnish, use either chisel-pointed bristle-brushes or badger-hair tools. For ordinary painting, such as lead, roughstuff, slush, etc., use either the round or oval varnish-brush, for these lay the paint more evenly and wear better, while the common paint-brush such as used by house painters, is not so economical.

Tuesday, 20.

"I DID NOT THINK."—But you should think; for that purpose were your faculties bestowed upon you. A thoughtless person is of necessity coarse and selfish. When people do wrong to their neighbors, and give pain unnecessarily, to say, "I did not think," puts forward no plea for tolerance, but is rather a reason for condemnation, and an additional peg on which to hang a sermon of rebuke. They should have thought; there is no good reason why they did not think; and, if they did not, then they did wrong, and wrong is always wrong and reprehensible.

Wednesday, 21.

STRIPING COLOR CUPS.—We frequently see small cups made by bending up pieces of sandpaper, and although these answer a very good purpose, they are not economical nor fully up to the requirements, for much of the liquid parts of the paint is absorbed by the paper. The best improvised vessels for holding paint in small quantities that we know of are the common hard shell of clams. These may be had for the asking, and when no longer required thrown away, and a new, clean one be substituted. A bushel of these should be kept on hand at all times, they cost nothing, and occupy but little room.

Thursday, 22.

A MILWAUKEE belle, attending a theatre in this city, complained in one of the scenes that the light was too dim to show the acting properly.

"Won't you try this glass?" asked her escort, handing her his lorgnette. Hastily covering the suspicious-looking object with her handkerchief, she placed it to her lips, took a long pull, and then handed it back in great disgust, saying: "Why, there ain't a drop in it."

Friday, 23.

PAINT CUPS.—The tin cups used to hold ground paints may be easily prepared for shop use. The patent can in which Valentine's Ivory Black is put up, has, when properly opened, a smooth edge and a nicely-fitting cover. To improve these and make complete, just solder a handle on one side and you have a convenient and economical paint-cup.

Saturday, 24.

Don Piatt's house in Washington took fire one Sunday morning. He superintended in person the moving out of his parlor furniture. The men carried a piano down the front steps and placed it on the sidewalk. "Here, boys," said Don, "don't leave that there, or the firemen will play on it."

Monday, 26.

DISHES FOR FINE COLORS.—Metal cups or dishes are well enough for most colors, but for vermilion, carmine, fine greens, lakes, earthen dishes are best. Earthen dishes are also excellent for varnish, owing to the ease with which they can be cleaned.

Tuesday, 27.

Use White Lead as sparingly as possible. There is no doubt that lead finds its way into the human body, under certain conditions, and there produces a variety of morbid changes, which may in some instances terminate in death; for the metal has often been found after death in the muscles, liver, brain, and other organs. White lead paint is introduced into the body in three ways: First, by the lungs. This takes place chiefly among house painters, when the lead is mixed with turpentine in large quantities. In the evaporation of the latter, a small amount of lead is carried off, and is breathed into the lungs. Lead dust may be taken in the same way by children and others, in the room where the work is being done. The second way is by direct absorption through the skin. The third method is by the mouth. When the painter is careless about his personal cleanliness, and neglects to change his clothing at meal time, a considerable quantity of paint may be taken into the bodies of those near him with their food and drink. This is especially true of the mid-day meal, which in many cases is eaten on the spot where the painter's work is going on.

Wednesday, 28.

PICKING OUT DUST, ETC.—When laying a coat of varnish upon a panel, spread on the necessary amount as evenly as possible, brush it across once to level it, then let it set for, say, two minutes; in that time the dust, if any, will show itself, and this is the time to "pick off." Don't wait until the varnish is *set* and the last dressing has been given, as some do, but go at it *now*, and with a sharpened whalebone or stick, or a quill—anything elastic and sharp-pointed—pick out every speck, then lay off or dress the varnish by crossing over it once or twice with light strokes of the brush.

Thursday, 29.

DUSTING OFF A JOB.—To thoroughly clean a body panel is, we know, a very nice operation, and one of the best plans for doing it is, after the work has been rubbed and washed as clean as sponges, water-tool, chamois and water will do it, to slightly dampen the extreme ends of the dusting-brush with varnish, and this is done by rubbing a little varnish upon the palm of the hand, and then gently rubbing the brush over it. This gives an adhesive property to the brush, and every little speck of lint or dust will be taken up by it, and the panel left as clean as it can possibly be made for the application of varnish.

Friday, 30.

Copy was out. The devil picked up a paper and said: "Here's something 'About a Woman'—must I cut it out?" "No!" thundered the editor; "the first disturbance ever created in the world was occasioned by the devil fooling about a woman."

1880 MAY. 1880

"He who paints with bristle or hair
Should of his colors have a care."

Sun.	Mon.	Tue.	Wed.	Thu.	Fri.	Sat.
--	--	--	--	--	--	1
2	3	4	5	6	7	8
9	10	11	12	13	14	15
16	17	18	19	20	21	22
23	24	25	26	27	28	29
30	31	--	--	--	--	--

Saturday, 1.

NEVER GIVE UP!

Fair fortune is a fickle dame—
She smiles on you to-day,
To-morrow turns her back on you,
And goes your neighbor's way.
Fret not, but still enjoy the good
That comes your way, though small—
Fly low, and if your wings be clipped,
You've not so far to fall.

Monday, 3.

A FEW years ago an unskilled workman was employed in the carriage department of one of the great railway companies. Last year that man was appointed superintendent of the car shops, where from three to four hundred workmen are commonly employed. That man always had the habit of carefully examining all that came under his observation, and looking back from effects to causes. Result: he now has a salary of £400 per year, equivalent in the town where he lives to $4,000 or $5,000 in New York city. Not every man can be a foreman or superintendent, but mechanics would do well to make greater efforts to qualify themselves for the position than they commonly do. Such efforts would give them a higher and better tone, and a more efficient mode of doing work. There are some persons who claim there are peculiarities about skilled mechanics which unfit them for responsible positions over their fellow workmen, and every day we see inferior workmen raised to places of trust. But you may be sure that carriage-makers infinitely prefer to have practical foremen and superintendents, men who know the wherefore of all that goes on in the shop, and who have the practical experience enabling them to correct any errors that occur—if they can only find in combination, in individuals, these two qualities: *mechanical skill and the power of management.*

Tuesday, 4.

WHERE is paper money first mentioned in the Bible ? When the dove brought *green back* to Noah.

A COAT of color—the one presented to Joseph by Jacob, his father.

Wednesday, 5.

WHITE WORK.—There seems to be a misunderstanding in regard to the varnish for work which is painted white, many relying upon white Damar varnish in order to keep the pure white color ; others, with the knowledge that the Damar varnish is not durable, thin down a light-colored carriage or copal varnish with turpentine, and apply it in a sparse manner for the same purpose. Now it has been demonstrated by practice that a white job will look better, wear longer, and give better satisfaction in every way when finished in " egg-shell gloss," and this is done in the following manner : After the job has been colored with one or more coats of pure white, mix and apply as color-and-varnish, either pure white lead or zinc (dry) in Valentine's Hard-Drying Body Varnish ; give ample time for drying ; then rub down with fine pumice-stone, and apply a second coat of same, adding a little more varnish, but not enough to materially affect the whiteness of the color-and-varnish. When dry, rub lightly with pulverized pumice, wash clean, and then rub nicely every part, being careful to have all

MAY, 1880.

parts look alike as regards luster, using pulverized rotten-stone in the place of pumice-stone. This gives the egg-shell finish to the surface. If striping or ornamenting is desired, this may be now put on with glossy color (not dead), and when dry, pencil-varnish over with Hard-Drying Body Varnish.

In case there is plenty of time at disposal, and the job must be a *very* durable one, use Valentine's Wearing Body Varnish in place of the H. D. B. varnish. However, the latter will make an excellent job, and quite durable enough for most work.

Thursday, 6.

"WHERE the labor and expense of producing a commodity is known to both parties, the bargain will generally be fair and equal. Where they are known to one party only, the bargain will often be unequal, knowledge taking its advantage of ignorance."—*B. Franklin.*

Friday, 7.

THE trouble experienced with paint chipping from the edges of springs and tires may be prevented by following these few simple rules: First, prime the wood and iron with P. W. F., and wipe off with rags. Then, when applying other coatings, be particular to *wipe off all the paint* from those parts which give trouble, and when *coloring* the job, lay the color on those parts very thin. Avoid, also, color-and-varnish coats over these parts. When the job is completed, there should be only one coat of priming, one coat of color, and one of varnish upon the edges of springs and tires, and these should remain intact as long as the other painted parts.

Saturday, 8.

THE first step toward education is the cultivation of a receptive mind. He who is best calculated to teach is most willing to learn ; and no one is warranted in being the preceptor of others who is not himself *still a scholar*. A prominent manufacturer once remarked in our hearing : "I never had an apprentice in my employ from whom I could not learn something."

Monday, 10.

FROST CRACKS.—When a carriage is run out of the shop with the paint and varnish not yet thoroughly *hard*—and this will be the case until the job has stood some weeks in the shop—the action of frozen water or mud upon the surface of the paint will be similar to that where quick-drying color is put over a surface of paint or varnish not quite dry—giving it the appearance of large or small cracks in proportion to the hardness of the frozen mud, the length of time it is in contact, or the state of the painted surface when exposed.

The mud not only draws a portion of the oil from the varnish, but it contracts and expands with heat and cold. We often see a wooden vessel or lead pipe burst by the force of frozen water, and it is said to be *expansion* which causes it. Now, if water or mud secures a hold upon a varnished or painted surface, which is elastic only to a certain extent, it will, when acted upon by cold, expand, and, instead of slipping or moving *over* the paint to which it adheres, it carries the paint with it as it congeals into a frozen mass. The consequence is, that when the mud or ice is removed cracks are found in the surface of the paint, sometimes to the extreme depth or thickness of that paint.

Tuesday, 11.

LIFE, to be worthy of a rational being, must be always in progression; we must always purpose to do more or better than in past times. The mind is enlarged and elevated by mere purposes, though they end as they begun, by airy contemplation. We compare and judge, though we do not practice.—*Dr. Samuel Johnson.*

Wednesday, 12.

HARD WATER.—Many of the troubles that beset the painter may be traced to the water used in rubbing and washing his work. Very hard or salt water, or water impregnated with lime, or with urine from stables, will seriously affect varnish; and the water running from a dye-house, which is probably impregnated with alum or alkali, should certainly be avoided. Rain water is best for washing varnish, and we would advise a large cask to hold the rain water from the roof of the shop where practicable.

Though insoluble in pure water, carbonate of lime is slightly·soluble in water which is already charged with carbonic acid ; and as all rain water brings down carbonic acid from the air, it is capable of taking up carbonate of lime from the soil and rocks through which it filters; and it thus happens that all water, rising in calcareous rock districts, is more or less charged with carbonate of lime, kept in solution by an excess of carbonic acid. This gives water that character known as "hardness." To avoid this source of trouble, simply *add a little lime-water*, which, by combining with the excess of carbonic acid, causes the precipitation of all the lime in solution in the form of insoluble carbonate, which settles to the bottom, leaving the water clear and soft.

Thursday, 13.

WE labor too much to *abolish*, too little to *utilize*.

It is easy to labor so long as we are encouraged by cheers and waving of hats, but to toil on and on, with only the silent approval of one's own heart, requires a noble fortitude which the hero alone possesses.

Friday, 14.

PARIS GREEN.—Paris green is a poor color to mix or work, and is not so frequently used as it otherwise would be on account of several peculiarities, one of which is its coarse, sandy appearance when mixed without grinding, and when ground fine, its luster and beauty are diminished, for reasons which Mr. Masury has explained. It may be mixed as follows : Mix one pound of dry color with one part of gold-size dryer, two parts rubbing varnish, and three parts raw oil ; add one ounce of sugar of lead, well pulverized, and grind in the mill. A little turpentine may be added, to allow it to grind easily and to thin it for working. The groundwork must be solid, for Paris green is transparent, and will show imperfections beneath it. A ground made with chrome green and white is preferred by most painters. Paris green is sometimes used as a glazing over other greens, as in lettering or ornamenting ; in such cases grind the dry color in Hard-Drying Body Varnish and a little oil.

Saturday, 15.

A FEW work with the pick-axe upon the hard quartz, slowly and laboriously, while the crowd scour the surface and depart satisfied ; when suddenly, on some lowering night-fall, the great mass falls and crumbles to pieces at the feet of the patient worker, yielding its reward of golden nuggets.

Monday, 17.

THE USE OF TOO MUCH DRYER IN PAINT.—"Too much of a good thing is good for nothing" is well said in the case of adding dryers such as Japan or Japan Gold-size to paint. *Too much* is liable to make the paint brittle and easily chipped off. *Too much* makes the paint porous, drying dead or flat; it absorbs the oils of the varnish and lessens its durability. *Too much* sometimes makes the paint saponaceous or soapy and anti-drying. *Too much* causes waste. Look to it, then, and never add more dryers to paint than sufficient to dry it in proper time; *too much* won't do.

Tuesday, 18.

FULLY one half of the unhappy people are so because they *think* that they are, or ought to be.

THE happiness or hardship of one's condition depends not so much on what it really is, as what one considers it to be. The kings of this world live most often in cottages.

Wednesday, 19.

TAKE CARE OF THE SURFACE.—Many painters seem to suppose that a slight run or a few brush marks in the coloring will do no harm; but that is a decided mistake, because it spoils a surface you have labored so hard to make, and, besides that, it leads one into the habit of carelessness. You make your surface "according to Hoyle" as the saying is, then, by using little care in subsequent operations, you spoil it. Be careful of the surface. Let each coat of color or varnish be laid on smoothly and, my word for it, you will never regret it.

Thursday, 20.

IT is a characteristic trait that the majority of people will laboriously climb over an obstacle in their path three times a day for as many months, before they think of removing it. And even then, it is so easy to say : "To-morrow I will see to that !"

MAY, 1880.

Friday, 21.

PARIS GREEN.—This is one of the most difficult pigments to manage that the painter is called upon to use. The mill in which it is ground, the cup in which it is held, the brush with which it is applied, must be perfectly clean, or a satisfactory result will not be obtained.

Mix as follows : Take one pound of dry color and add one ounce of pulverized sugar of lead, mix in four parts raw oil, two parts rubbing varnish ("Elastic" or "Quick Leveling"), and one part Japan Goldsize, thin with turpentine when grinding and when applying, if found too *thick*.

Saturday, 22.

HAVING ten things to do, it is much better to perform five, and leave the others unattempted, than to half-do or mis-do the ten. In one case, *something* has been accomplished, even though little ; in the other, we may have done worse than nothing.

Monday, 24.

IMITATION GROUND GLASS.—To make imitation ground glass that steam will not destroy, put a piece of putty in muslin, twist the fabric tight, and tie it into the shape of a pad ; well clean the glass first, and then pat it all over. The putty will exude sufficiently through the muslin to render the stain opaque. Let it dry hard, and then varnish. If a pattern is required, cut it out in paper as a stencil, place it so as not to slip, and proceed as above, removing the stencil when finished. If there should be any objection to the existence of the clear spaces, cover with slightly opaque varnish.

Tuesday, 25.

ALTHOUGH it is wise to give main strength to your own speciality, you should not confine yourself to such studies exclusively. The perfection of all your powers should be your aspiration. Those who can only think and talk on one subject may be efficient in their line, but they are not agreeable members of society in any of its departments. Neither have they made the most of themselves. They become one-sided and narrow in their views, and are reduced to a humiliating dependence on one branch of industry. It costs nothing to carry knowledge, and in times like these to be able to put his hand to more than one branch of industry, often serves a man a good turn.

Wednesday, 26.

FOR the painting of floors with oil-paint, we should only select such as contain earthy coloring substances, and no lead, as all paints containing the latter wear off too easily.

A floor that is covered with oil-paint, and which is comparatively easily rubbed off. can safely be considered to contain lead.

Lead is generally added on account of its superior density, body, and also being much more easily applied than most other substances.

Even varnish that has been prepared by the use of litharge is objectionable on account of being too readily worn off.

Two coats of paint are usually employed, and care should be observed so as not to apply the second before the first is fully dry.

Thursday, 27.

THE best education one can obtain is the education experience gives. In passing through life learn everything you can. It will all come in play. Don't be frightened away from any pursuit because you have only a little time to devote to it. If you can't have any more, a smattering is infinitely better than nothing. Even a slight knowledge of the arts, sciences, languages, opens up a whole world of thought. A little systematic endeavor—one hour, or ever half an hour, a day—and a man may be considered learned before he dies. Learn thoroughly what you learn, be it ever so little, and you may speak of it with confidence. A few clearly-defined facts and ideas are worth a whole library of uncertain knowledge.

Friday, 28.

DARKENING OF VERMILION.—The darkening of vermilion occurs not so much from impure pigment as from the imperfect manipulation by the painter. Sunlight exerts an influence upon it, but, providing the color is properly mixed and applied, it will withstand this influence a long time. If a darkened vermilion surface be scraped with a knife, the color, underneath a thin shell of gum, will be found perfect—as in the case of black turning green. Now the question arises,

MAY, 1880.

what is this *gum* or dark film? and our answer is—*the vehicles of the paint.*

Saturday, 29.

A CARRIAGE-painter cannot make a good job unless he has a good surface to work on, nor can he be a good painter unless he understands thoroughly the first principles of his trade. Be satisfied to do or learn one thing at a time; the world is made up of atoms. When you learn a thing, be sure you know it, for a little well done is better than much poorly accomplished.

Monday, 31.

AMONG the most pleasing colors which harmonize with each other in pairs, are:

Blue and gold.	Blue and orange.
Purple and gold.	Blue and scarlet.
Green and gold.	Blue and black.
Black and gold.	Blue and white.
Crimson and gold.	Blue and chestnut.
Brown and gold,	Chestnut and orange.
Brown and orange.	Green and orange.

THE DIFFERENCE BETWEEN COMBINING AND MIXING.—When different ingredients are mingled together without undergoing any chemical change, they are said to be mixed; but when the natural properties of each are altered by the union, then those ingredients are said to be combined. The painter makes various mixtures and but few combinations. When he takes red and yellow, and produces the hue called orange, or blue and yellow and forms green, he has mingled two colors which remain distinct, although they are not visible to the naked eye.

When he applies ammonia (not alkali) to the varnish on an old body, in order to soften it, he produces a combination. The ammonia combines with the oil of the varnish, and the properties of each are changed and form a soapy compound having slight adhesiveness, which is easily removed with the putty knife.

Sometimes the varnish on an old body resists the action of ammonia. This is from the fact that the oily substance is dried out of the varnish, leaving only the resinous part behind.

1880   JUNE.   1880

"Look well to your priming
And never desert your colors!"—*Gardner.*

Sun.	Mon.	Tue.	Wed.	Thu.	Fri.	Sat.
--	--	1	2	3	4	5
6	7	8	9	10	11	12
13	14	15	16	17	18	19
20	21	22	23	24	25	26
27	28	29	30	--	--	--
--	--	--	--	--	--	--

Tuesday, 1.

TURNING OVER THE NEW LEAF.

The year begins. I turn a leaf,
  All over writ with good resolves;
Each to fulfil will be in chief
  My aim while earth its round revolves.
How many a leaf I've turned before,
  And tried to make the record true;
Each year a wreck on time's dull shore
  Proved much I dared, but little knew.

Wednesday, 2.

THE months of June, July and August are to the painter the most trying ones of the year. The "deviltries" caused by extreme heat will frequently vex him, and no doubt call out anathemas on the varnish maker, when that often berated individual is entirely innocent of wrong doing. The most troublesome, or, at least, the most frequent "deviltry" during the heated term is that known as "sweating." We do not speak of perspiration which heat or hard labor brings out upon the brow of the toiler, but the return of the gloss upon a varnished surface, after it has been removed from the varnish by rubbing with pumice-stone and water. This "sweating" of a coat of varnish is the cause of pitting, enameling, silking, and several other deviltries, and it is to some painters *a terrible visitor*. Now, to silence forever the cry of "sweating" and make with one swoop a death-blow to the bug-bear (for it is that and nothing more), we exhort the painter to follow these simple directions :

First.—Apply all varnish coats with a medium degree of thickness—not *too heavy*.

Second.—Lay each coat as evenly and as clean as if it was to be the finish.

Third.—Give a reasonable time for drying, then simply "flat" the surface. Do not rub the varnished surface too much.

Fourth.—Wash the job clean, and IMMEDIATELY apply the varnish. Do not let the work stand a half-hour—"put on the varnish right away," and our word for it, the troubles of "sweating" will be overcome.

A resinous, hard-drying, inelastic varnish will not "sweat" easily, and many use such a one, depending upon a good finishing varnish to protect it, but such work is not durable. There is no perfect assimilation between the coats applied, and where this is not present no wearing qualities exist.

USE A GOOD QUALITY OF ELASTIC VARNISH, RUB LIGHTLY, AND VARNISH IMMEDIATELY AFTER RUBBING.

Thursday, 3.

YOU are more sure of success in the end if you regard yourself as a man of ordinary talent, with plenty of hard work before you, than if you think yourself a man of genius and spend too much time in watching your hair grow long, that you may convince people that you are not like other folk.

A CLERGYMAN had a milk-white horse, which on account of its beautiful form he called Zion. Having ordered his horse, a friend asked him where he was going. "Why," said he "to *mount Zion*."

JUNE, 1880.

Friday, 4.
IMPORTANT FEATURES IN PAINTING.

VARNISHES.—The importance of employing materials throughout a job of painting that will harmonize one with the other, is sometimes overlooked, and we think it quite proper to describe briefly the varnishes which may be used in the "American Method of Carriage Painting" with absolute safety as regards their assimilation with the under coats of paint, while the world-wide reputation of these goods (Valentine's Varnishes) prevents us from extending our remarks thereon. Read the list carefully.

Saturday, 5.

WEARING BODY VARNISH.—This varnish is made of the best materials the inventive genius of man can compound. It is designed for the final or finishing coat over carriage bodies, is pale in color, and exceedingly limpid, so that it works well under the brush and possesses that quality so much admired by the varnisher, and known as "thickening under the brush," in order that a heavy coat may be laid upon a panel without fear of its running down in festoons or clouds and heavy masses. It is the *king* of all varnishes made, *i.e.*, the best, most durable, brilliant, and therefore valued at the highest price of varnishes. This varnish is less liable to turn blue by reason of dampness than most finishing varnishes.

Monday, 7.

MEDIUM DRYING BODY VARNISH.—This varnish is next in grade to the Wearing Body Varnish, the only difference being in its drying qualities. It dries and hardens more quickly, rendering it better adapted for tropical climates or for use in hot weather in the temperate zone. It is used upon carriage bodies mostly, although it may be applied to gears when desired. This varnish is preferable for painters who are obliged to work in unclean shops, on account of its drying out of the way of dust quickly.

Tuesday, 8.

ELASTIC GEAR VARNISH.—This varnish is made more particularly for the wheels and under parts of a carriage, and although possessing a large share of elasticity, will dry in from eight to ten hours sufficiently hard for handling. One coat of this varnish over a well made foundation will give extreme durability. Like the Wearing Body Varnish it works nicely under the brush, and the painter may easily lay it over a wheel before giving it the final "dressing" or laying off.

Wednesday, 9.

ELASTIC LEVELING VARNISH.—This varnish is similar to the Hard-Drying Body Varnish, but is made to dry and harden for rubbing quicker. It is fully equal to the H. D. B. in paleness and ease in working.

Thursday, 10.

QUICK LEVELING VARNISH.—This varnish dries quicker and harder than either of the other rubbing varnishes mentioned, and for hurried work is just the requirement. It is an excellent varnish for inside house work or for furniture, or in any place where hard and quick drying is required. It is pale and limpid, and is much used for color-and-varnish coats on cheap work.

Friday, 11.

ENAMELED LEATHER VARNISH.—This is a preparation for giving leather that appearance it had when new. It dries very quickly and should be used as follows: First clean the leather thoroughly with soap and water, and when dry, if soft and pliable, put on at once a thin coating of this dressing, using a medium-size bristle brush. Should the leather be very hard, old and stiff, apply just a coating of our Dark Permanent Wood Filling with a brush and sponge, and *wipe well with rags* so as to leave no P. W. F. on the surface. Let stand over night to dry; then apply a coat of this Dressing, which will dry in an hour or so ready for use. This varnish may also be used as a staining over oak-grained wood-work in houses, to give a black-walnut appearance to the same.

Saturday, 12.

RAILWAY COACH FINISHING VARNISH.—This is to the car painter what Wearing Body is to the carriage painter—the best quality of varnish for the exterior of railroad cars. It is the custom of car painters now-a-days to apply two coats of this varnish, instead of more rubbing coats. A good washing and a drying with a chamois will prepare the surface for the second coat, providing it be applied immediately and before any sweating of the surface begins. This adds greatly to the durability of the work.

Monday, 14.

INSIDE COACH FINISHING VARNISH.—This varnish is intended for the finishing coats on car interiors and where great dispatch is necessary one coat over a surface made by Inside Rubbing Varnish will answer well, but it is recommended in ordinary cases to flow on two coats in the same manner as mentioned for the outside of the car. A car finished with these varnishes will only require a single coat of the same annually to preserve the paint for years. How often we see cars, painted at the expense of several hundred dollars, almost denuded of their paint in a few months, because varnished with an insufficient number of coats, or with an article lacking in durability—thus causing a total loss of both paint and varnish, and of the time and labor spent in applying them, when an application, at the outset, of enough coats of a durable varnish, *with the renewal of a single coat each year*, would have preserved both wood and paint as long as the car held together.

Tuesday, 15.

ONE COAT COACH VARNISH.—This is a heavier-bodied varnish than the usual finishing varnishes, and is intended for finishing work where a single coat only is practicable, as, for instance, the revarnishing of a livery-stable job or hack, and for cheap work, where a few coats of paint or varnish saved is a consideration. It possesses very excellent qualities of brilliancy and durability, and gives general satisfaction wherever used.

Wednesday, 16.

HARD DRYING BODY VARNISH.—This is the finest quality of rubbing varnish made. It is fully equal to the above mentioned finishing varnishes in paleness, fullness, and luster, and is frequently used for finishing hurried work. It works well under the brush, and in 48 hours may be rubbed with pulverized pumice-stone and water preparatory to receiving a finishing coat. Although intended for carriage bodies, it is one of the best ingredients for color-and-varnish on either bodies or gears, and for use in some paints or for glazings, particularly for white work.

Thursday, 17.

LOCOMOTIVES, being varnished more frequently than cars, and the varnish upon them being protected somewhat by the oil from the " waste " used in cleaning them, do not require so durable an article as Railway Coach Finishing, and usually sufficient time cannot be given for it to dry ; we therefore commend for this work Locomotive Finishing in place of it. The dispensing with a quicker varnish for under coats is just as desirable on the inside as on the outside work of cars, and because of the increased durability, we recommend the use of Inside Coach Finishing for all the coats inside of cars, and Locomotive Finishing for all the coats on Locomotives and Tenders when time can be taken ; but, when *dispatch* is indispensable, or of more importance than durability, many use Inside Coach Rubbing and Locomotive Rubbing for the under coats.

Friday, 18.

CRACKING.—To prevent color-coats from cracking, use Japan Gold-size (an oil drier) ; which, being a binder and hardener, as well as a dryer of great strength, is less detrimental than common shellac Japans, but half the quantity being required. If you observe the work in a steam or horse-car, it will commonly be found cracked, and a careful examination will generally show the cause to be in the paint, or, on unpainted work, in the brittle undercoats of varnish, used to fill the pores and to level over. This can be avoided by mixing the color-coats with Japan Gold-size. This article is peculiarly valuable on Railway work, where light colors are used, because of its paleness and the small quantity required.

Saturday, 19.

" *TOUCHING UP.*"—Many painters are disinclined to use Black Japan on account, as they say, of trouble in matching the jet black if a spot is rubbed through and " touching up " is necessary. Now this is all *bosh*. In the first place the job should be—at the time for the last coat of varnish—so level, and so well rubbed, that no rubbing through or touching up places are to be seen. However, accident may cause these places, and to "touch up," first go over with a thin coat of quick Ivory Black, then with common asphaltum—which can be procured at any paint store—thinned down with turpentine and put on with a small camel's-hair brush, the spot will appear the same in color as other parts of the job.

Monday, 21.

SPECKS IN VARNISH.—The painter will say to us sometimes: "In using my finishing varnishes my carriage bodies appear to be all full of little specks. I have strained my varnish thoroughly, but all to no purpose; please tell me what is the cause of this, so that I may remedy the evil." We answer: specks in a coat of varnish are caused by *cold*, as when the can containing the varnish has been left in an exposed position, or when the room or the panels are cold; also, by *turpentine*, if the brushes were rinsed out or suspended in turpentine. A trifling amount only is sufficient to spoil a cup full of varnish.

Tuesday, 22.

FLIES.—These pests to the painter are kept in the minority to a great extent by keeping the paint-rooms, and especially the varnish-room, *dark*. Camphor-gum placed around on window-ledges and out-of-the-way places is also a preventive against the swarming of small gnats, flies, millers, etc., and as it is quite inexpensive, a good supply should always be on hand.

Wednesday, 23.

HARD-WOOD FINISHING. There is much hard-wood finishing to be done on heavy work, such as card-cases, stable shutters, etc., and these should be *polished*. Take Valentine's Quick Leveling Varnish, and after applying from four to five coats, giving time between each coat for drying, rub down well first with pumice-stone, then with rotten-stone, and lastly with sweet oil and rotten-stone mixed. For inside fittings that are to be in imitation of ebony, soak the wood in a decoction of logwood, then in another of vinegar and iron-rust, and rub to a smooth surface with fine emery-paper.

Thursday, 24.

INSIDE FITTINGS.—The card-cases, mirrors, and other inside fittings of a close carriage are frequently made of maple or soft wood and then deyd to imitate ebony, and this ebony finish is simply the common black stain made from the same ingredients as common ink. A solution of sulphate of iron, green vitriol or copperas, which is all the same thing, is washed two or three times over the wood, letting it dry each time, then a strong decoction of logwood is passed hot over it, also two or three times; when dry, wipe with a sponge and cold water, rub well with linseed oil, and finally polish, either in the French way or with the brush.

Friday, 25.

CHOICE OF HAIR TOOLS.—Round and flat brushes are used, but the flat are more useful. They should be neatly made and yet very strong, and the hair should not be cut at the points, but smooth to the touch. They should also be very elastic, springing back to their shape when in use, and the hair should be silky-looking. There should be no diverging hairs, but their shape should be wedge-like. Polished cedar handles ensure thorough cleaning, and they are more pleasant to use. Sable tools should come to a firm, fine point, and the hair must be of a pale yellow cast. They can be had both flat and round. Badger tools are superior when the hair is light, long and pliant; in color black, with white ends. Instead of coming to a point, the hairs diverge. They seldom want cleaning, as used by gilders.

Saturday, 26.

SWEATING OF VARNISH COATS.—*Definition.*—The greasy gloss which makes its appearance upon a varnished surface, after it has been rubbed with pumice-stone and water, then allowed to stand for some time.

Causes.—1. When varnish is applied over color or color-and-varnish that is not thoroughly dry, it seals up and prevents the hardening of that under-coating, and the drying process is delayed for a length of time beyond that generally given for the varnish to harden; then, if rubbed, this drying out process goes on and is made visible by a partial return of the luster or gloss.

2. When varnish—although put over a well-dried surface—is laid on too heavy, or put on in patches and not uniform all over the work, it will not harden well, and when rubbed will "sweat" in parts of the work.

3. When varnish is *rubbed too much*, that is, rubbed nearly all off, that which remains upon the work, not being hard, will sweat, if allowed to stand a while.

4. Sweating is therefore nothing more than evidence that the drying process is still going on, and proves that the varnish or the under coats are not yet hard or dry.

Effects.—The effect upon a coat of varnish applied over a sweated surface is to produce small indentations or pin-holes all over the work, or to cause the varnish to appear rough, like enameled leather, or streaked, as the threads of silk, technically called "pitting," "pin-holing," "enameling," "silking," etc.

Remarks.—Although "sweating" occasions, at times, great trouble and expense, and is the cause of much poor work, the painter need have no trouble from it *if he will do his work in a proper manner!* Sweating is of NO CONSEQUENCE if the job be rightly treated.

The fact that the under coats or that the varnish is not thoroughly hard and dry, need not disturb the painter, for if varnish be applied to the rubbed surface before the sweating makes its appearance (and there is always time enough to do this) no deviltry will occur.

The great trouble is, painters are too apt to be careless with their rubbing coats and "pile on more than enough," or else have it well sprinkled with dust and hairs from the brush, saying: "No matter, it has yet to be rubbed," and when the rubbing time comes, there is a good deal of *rubbing* to be done in order to get the "nibs" out and to make the work smooth. Now, this is all wrong; such men can make a good job—in appearance—with a hard furniture varnish, but with a good, durable varnish they are incompetent. And it is no wonder that work which ought to be durable because of its good foundation and good material in the finish, is found to decay rapidly when a hard rubbing varnish *that* NEVER *sweats* is used simply because a fear of the effects of sweating in a *real good* varnish is entertained. It is like making a sandwich of good bread and rotten meat.

Sweating, and the deviltries it produces, are bug-bears easily driven away.

Lay on your varnish coats as if every one of them were for the finish.

Rub the surface, after a reasonable time, just sufficient to "flat it."

Wash the job clean with cold water, dry off well with a chamois, and apply the next coat IMMEDIATELY.

Do not allow the job to stand even a half hour before varnishing, and sweating will be an obsolete term, used only by painters who don't know their business.

Monday, 28.

SWEATING OF VARNISH COATS.—Poor, resinous varnishes will not "sweat."

Good, elastic and durable varnishes *will* sweat, when not thoroughly dry, after the surface is rubbed with pumice-stone and water.

"Sweating" does not impair the work, but the troubles arising from it, such as "pitting," "enameling," etc., are to be deplored. *Therefore*, to prevent the "sweating" of a surface, the painter should apply the varnish coat IMMEDIATELY after the rubbing and cleansing of the work.

"WHAT THE EYE DON'T SEE THE HEART WON'T GRIEVE FOR."

If you never allow a job to stand after it has been rubbed down with pumice-stone and water, you will never *see* "sweating," and consequently have no such deviltries occurring in your shop as "crawling," "pitting," etc., which are caused by sweating.

"THIS VARNISH DOES NOT 'SWEAT!'"

No, it is a hard, inelastic, resinous varnish, and will not "sweat," causing "pitting," "enameling," etc., and if you do not put a good finishing varnish over it, it will not be very durable. Why are you afraid of a sweating varnish? You need not let it "sweat." No occasion for it whatever. It's all nonsense to say the body is ruined on account of *sweating of the varnish!* Rub the surface lightly and lay the varnish on IMMEDIATELY. Don't stand like an idiot looking at the job until the "sweat" comes out on the surface, and you need never know what "sweating" is.

Tuesday, 29.

You cannot make yourself better by simply resolving to be better at some time or other, any more than a farmer can plough his field by simply turning it over in his own mind. A good resolution is a fine starting point, but as a terminus it has no value.

JUNE, 1880.

Wednesday, 30.

This day brings us to the end of the almanac, and ere I bid adieu to my readers, I wish to say : That should there be any point discovered, or any statement made in the practical portions of my book which conflicts with the experience of the reader, it would please me, as well as be a source of information, if he will write me his views thereon ; and if he be pleased or benefited in any manner by perusing these pages, I ask as a favor that he drop me a postal card stating such fact.

Address   The Author.
    323 Pearl-st.,
        New-York.

PAINTING A WHITE JOB.

To paint a white sleigh by the "American method." First, dust off the body, and with a clean brush apply a coat of P. W. F., using no particular care to have it lay nicely. Daub it on, we might say. Then proceed to wipe off all superfluous P. W. F. That is, do not allow anything like a surface coat as of varnish or paint to remain. Wipe it as dry as possible. A sufficient amount of P. W. F. will have penetrated the surface to insure good results. Next, stand the job aside to dry for forty-eight hours. When this time has passed, lay on a coat of Valentine's Light Roughstuff as smoothly as possible ; and here let us remark, the smoother the foundation coats are laid, and the less number of brush marks left in sight the smoother will be the finish, and the less labor it will entail upon the operator.

The first coat of roughstuff should have a little oil added, say about five per cent. to make it harmonize with the P. W. F. properly. Then give it twenty-four hours for drying. When dry, putty up all the holes and imperfections in the surface, and apply the second coat of Valentine's Light Roughstuff, using no oil, but simply thinning it with turpentine to have it spread nicely. Give twenty-four hours for drying. Next completely fill all screw and nail holes with putty and lay on the third coat of roughstuff. The following day a coat of staining may be applied. This is simply some color, say Indian red mixed with Japan and turpentine, which will color the surface so that the rubber may easily see when he has rubbed the roughstuff sufficiently. This stain coat will dry rapidly, although it is best, when time is no object, to let the job stand for drying as long as possible.

Now rub down the rough stuff carefully; wash off clean, dry well, and set the job aside until the next day, in order that the water or moisture absorbed by the paint may evaporate.

Next, take the light shade P. W. F., it being a trifle thinner and easier to work, and apply a thin coating directly to the rubbed surface. This penetrates the porous paint, and effectually closes it against absorption, as well as giving the surface extra binding and elastic qualities. Wipe off as clean as rags will wipe it, and let it stand twenty-four hours. When this has been done the job is ready for color.

The color we mix as follows: Take keg-lead of good quality, and mix with turpentine a considerable more than wanted for the job in hand, to a thin, milky consistency. Allow it to set until a large portion of the lead has gone to the bottom, when the thin oil and turpentine found floating on top may be poured off. This is done to remove the excess of oil in the lead which would be detrimental to the paint as a color to be spread with a soft camel's-hair brush. When the lead has settled and the superabundant liquid poured off, take a small quantity of the lead and reduce it to a working consistency with turpentine, then add a tablespoonful of Japan gold-size to each pint of mixed paint. Stir well, and apply with a soft brush, leaving as few brush marks as possible. The next day apply a second coat of the same. The day following take some of the settled lead, and add to it some hard Drying Body Varnish to form color-and-varnish. Apply this with varnish brushes, and give from two to three days for drying. When dry, rub down nicely with pulverized stone and water, and apply a second coat of color and varnish, made by mixing zinc-white (oxide or zinc) with Wearing Body Varnish, in the same manner as before with mixing lead and varnish. One heavy flowing coat of this should make a clean and pure white job. Give three or four days to dry; then rub off all extra gloss or luster with pulverized rotten-stone and water, leaving the surface with an egg-shell gloss, and hang up the job.

If in eight or ten months this job shows signs of discoloration or decay (the latter is not probable) run the job into the shop and lightly rub with rotten-stone again; or if very much discolored, apply another finishing coat of zinc and varnish.

If striping or other ornamentation is desired, this should be done on the finished ground, and then pencil-varnished.

This plan of operation has invariably proved a success, and is highly recommended by the best painters in the United States.

RECEIPTS FOR MIXING COLORS.

WE furnish the following receipts for mixing colors more particularly required in painting carriages and sleighs. The proportions are not, of course, arbitrary, and it would be impossible to make them so, for pigments are not always uniform, even when bearing the same name and general appearance. They will serve, however, as a good general guide, and any painter after a little experience will learn to change the proportions to suit either the strength of the pigments or his own taste:

French Red—This color is simply Indian red lightened with vermilion, and glazed with carmine.

Chocolate Color—Add a little lake or carmine to a pot of burnt umber; or take Indian red and black to form a brown; then add a very little yellow, to bring about the desired shade.

Yellow Lake—Take of umber and white equal parts, add a small quantity of Naples yellow and a drop of scarlet lake; glaze with yellow lake.

Olive Brown—Mix one part of lemon yellow with three parts of burnt umber. Change proportions for different shades.

Clay Drab—Raw sienna, raw umber, and white lead, equal parts; then tint with a few drops of chrome green.

Bismarck Brown—Take 1 ounce of carmine, ½ ounce crimson lake, and 1 ounce best gold bronze, and mix together. If a light shade is desired, use vermilion in place of carmine.

Jonquil Yellow—Mix flakewhite and chrome yellow, and add a very little vermilion or carmine.

Medium Gray—Eight parts of white to two of black.

Lead Color—Eight parts white, one of blue, and one of black.

Light Buff—Yellow ochre, lightened with white.

Deep Buff—The same, with the addition of a little red.

French Gray—White, tinted with Ivory Black.

Gold Color—White and yellow, tinted with red and blue.

Pearl Color—White, black and red, in proportion to suit taste of the painter.

Canary Color—White and lemon yellow, or patent yellow.

Oak Color—Eight parts of white, and one of yellow ochre.

Olive Color—Eight parts of yellow, one blue, and one black.

Snuff Color—Four parts of yellow, and two of Vandyke brown.

Rose Color—Five parts of white, and two of carmine.

Bottle Green—Dutch pink and Prussian blue for ground; glaze with yellow lake.

Salmon Color—Five parts of white, one yellow, one umber, one red.
Brown—Three parts of red, two black, and one yellow.
Copper Color—One part red, two of yellow, and one black.
Lemon Color—Five parts of lemon yellow, and two of white.
Straw Color—Five parts of yellow, two of white, and one of red.
Fawn Color—Eight parts of white, one of red, two yellow, and one umber.
Flesh Color—Eight parts of white, three of red, and three of chrome yellow.
Chestnut Color—Two parts of red, one black, and two chrome yellow.
Wine Color—Two parts of ultramarine, and three of carmine.
Green—Blue and yellow, or black and yellow.
Maroon Color—Three parts of carmine, and two of yellow.
Tan Color—Five parts of burnt sienna, two yellow, and one raw umber.
Pea Green—Five parts of white, and one of chrome green.
Stone Color—Five parts of white, two yellow, and one of burnt umber.
Citron—Three parts of red, two yellow, and one blue.
Drab Color—Nine parts of white, and one umber.
Lilac—Four parts of red, three white, and one blue.
Purple—The same as lilac, but differently proportioned; say, two parts of blue.
Violet—Similar, but more red in it than purple.
London Smoke—Two parts umber, one white, and one red.
Cream Color—Five parts white, two yellow, and one red.
Claret Color—Red and black, or carmine and blue.
Dove Color—Red, white, blue and yellow.
Light Gray—Nine parts white, one blue, and one black.
Willow Green—Five parts white, and two verdigris.
Peach Blossom—Eight parts white, one red, one blue, and one yellow.
Bronze Green—Five parts chrome green, one black, and one umber.
Carnation Red—Three parts lake, and one white.
Grass Green—Three parts yellow, and one Prussian blue.
Brick Color—Two parts yellow ochre, one red, and one white.
Portland Stone—Three parts raw umber, three yellow ochre, one white.
Plum Color—Two parts white, one blue, and one red.

INDEX.

	Page
THE AMERICAN METHOD OF CARRIAGE PAINTING	6
Priming with P. W. F.	6
Roughstuff	7
Putty	7
Applying roughstuff	7
Smoked and burned places	8
The last coat of roughstuff	8
Selecting pumice-stone	9
P. W. F. over the roughstuff	9
Color and varnish on gears	9
Coloring the body	9
Black Japan	10
Striping	10
Finishing the body	11
"Hanging up"	11
Mixing colors	14
Improving carriage tops	14
Greasy color	15
Clean varnish cups	15
A world within itself	16
The varnish-room floor	16
Black Japan	17
Permanent Wood Filling	17
Painter's rule	18
Chipped work	18
Varnish changing color	19
Japan Gold-size	19
Japan brown	20
Roughstuff	20
Weight of liquids	22
Rubbing coats	22
Dark rich brown	22
PAINTING SLEIGHS	23
Priming	23
Roughstuff	23
Colors	24
P. W. F. on wood and iron	24
Rubbing	24
Two coats of color	24
Color-and-varnish	25
Striping	25
Gilding	25
Varnishing	25
Transfer pictures	25
Color for sleighs	26
To mix tints	27
Artificial coral	27
Painting old work	28
General synopsis	28
Color-and-varnish	30

	Page
Gilding-size	30
How to keep paint brushes	31
Oiling work	32
Chamois skin	33
P. W. F. on rosewood	33
How to devise a new color	34
The drying on of pumice-stone	34
Japan Gold-size for gilding	35
P. W. F. for brick work	36
American vermilion	36
Ultramarine	37
Badly-chipped paint	37
Sweating of varnish	40
Cleaning varnish brushes	40
Hot water	40
Mixing varnishes	41
Varnish brushes	41
Varnishing Gold bronze	41
Finishing varnish	42
Keeping varnish brushes	43
Varnishing in summer	43
Rubbing cloths	43
Per centages in mixing	44
Staining oak graining	44
Concealing old cracks	45
A superficial finish	45
Cleanliness of the shop	46
Repainting	48
Prussian blue	48
PAINTING CHEAP WORK	49
Priming	49
Roughstuff	49
Putty	49
Shop marks	49
Burned places	50
Rubbing	50
P. W. F. over putty	50
Lampblack	50
Ivory Black	51
Rubbing gears	51
Flatting	51
Finishing	52
Hanging up	52
Polishing varnish	52
B. C. and V.	53
General rules	53
The deviltries of cold weather	56
The Hub Chart	56
How to rub out runs	57
Gold bronze	57
Sandpapering, etc	58

INDEX.

	Page
Prepared black	59
Keeping cups	60
Putty for glass frames	61
Formula for mixing paint	61
Cleanliness	62
Old pigment	62
Varnishing	63
Gilding-size	63
Priming	65
Painting zinc	66
Mixing varnishes	66
Chinese vermilion	67
Puttying	67
Rubbing through	68
White lead	68
Prepared roughstuff	69
Drying out	69
Ground colors	70
Cans for the bench	71
Synopsis of American Method	72
The deviltries of varnish	74
Polishing a body	75
The goods of several makers, etc.	75
Camel's-hair brushes	76
Brushes	76
Grinding pigments	77
Extreme heat and cold	77
Carmine	78
Showering carriages	78
Ultramarine	79
Paint on Brougham body	80
Water pails	80
Light ground roughstuff	81
Preparing for finishing	81
When shall we varnish?	83
The last coat of varnish	84
White lead	85
Blue and yellow	86
Blackboard paint	86
Pouncing ornaments	87
Elasticity on gears	87
Brushes	88
Striping color cups	88

	Page
Paint Cups	89
Dishes for fine colors	89
Use of lead	89
Picking out dust, etc	90
Dusting off a job	90
Foremen	91
White work	92
Paint chipping from springs	93
Frost cracks	94
Hard water	94
Paris green	95
Too much dryer	96
Take care of the surface	96
Paris green	97
Imitation ground glass	97
Painting floors	98
Darkening of vermilion	98
Harmony of colors	99
Combining and mixing	99
Rules for "sweating"	101
VARNISHES	103
Wearing Body Varnish	103
Medium Drying Body Varnish	103
Elastic Gear Varnish	103
Elastic Leveling Varnish	104
Quick Leveling Varnish	104
Enameled Leather Varnish	104
Railway Coach Finishing Varnish	104
Inside Coach Finishing Varnish	105
One-Coat Coach Varnish	105
Hard-Drying Body Varnish	105
Locomotive Varnish	106
Cracking	106
"Touching up"	106
Specks in varnish	107
Flies	107
Hard wood finishing	107
Inside fittings	108
Choice of hair tools	108
SWEATING OF VARNISH COATS	108
PAINTING A WHITE JOB	111
52 receipts for mixing colors	113

ERRATA.

On page 28, 6th line from bottom, for "give 16 hours," read give 6 hours.

www.ingramcontent.com/pod-product-compliance
Lightning Source LLC
Chambersburg PA
CBHW020136170426
43199CB00010B/773